Effective
Bible Teaching

Effective
Bible Teaching

Jim Wilhoit and Leland Ryken

BAKER BOOK HOUSE
Grand Rapids, Michigan 49516

Copyright 1988 by
Baker Book House Company

ISBN: 0-8010-9685-5

Fifth printing, March 1992

Printed in the United States of America

Library of Congress Cataloging-in-Publication Data

Wilhoit, Jim.
    Effective Bible teaching.

    Includes indexes.
    1. Bible—Study.   I. Ryken, Leland.   II. Title.
BS600.2.W55   1988   220'.07   88–16826
ISBN 0–8010–9685–5

To our students

Contents

10 What Kind of Book Is the Bible?   181
        A Collection of Books
        The Unity of the Bible
        A Book of Encounter
11 Types of Writing in the Bible   191
        An Overview of Biblical Genres
        The Bible as Literature
12 Teaching the Stories of the Bible   207
        The Challenge and Necessity of Teaching the
            Stories of the Bible
        The Descriptive Level: Setting, Characters, and
            Action
        From Story to Meaning
        Avoiding Some Common Pitfalls
13 Teaching the Poetry of the Bible   223
        Thinking in Images
        A Language of Comparison
        Poetry as a Form of Fiction
        How Poems Are Organized
14 Teaching Other Genres of the Bible   237
        The Proverb
        Satire
        Visionary Writing
        The Epistles
        The Parables

        Index of Subjects   251
        Index of Authors   255

Preface

From the time that Luther declared that "the entire life and being of the church lie in the word of God," Protestantism has committed itself to the tasks of preaching and teaching the Word. Of the two, preaching has fared better than teaching.

Bible teaching is the medium of neglect in the contemporary church. Seminaries have required courses in homiletics, and nearly every month brings the publication of a new book on preaching. But where are the books and courses on teaching the Bible? No wonder a Gallup poll uncovered people who believe the Bible to be God's inspired Word and yet cannot name four of the Ten Commandments. Effective Bible teaching heads the agenda of the church's unfinished tasks.

Part of the problem is that the church has failed to equip lay people to study and teach the Bible. Without intending to do so, it has handed over the task of interpreting the Bible to its ministers. Ministers themselves feel more comfortable in the pulpit than in front of a class. They lavish their time on their sermons and by comparison feel that anything is good enough when it comes to teaching the Bible.

Nor have ministers been quick to oversee that lay people teach the Bible effectively. Armed with a knowledge of the Bible's original languages, and having been initiated into the sophisticated world of modern biblical interpretation, most ministers simply do not know how to popularize the methods of technical biblical scholarship that they learned in seminary. "How can I pass on in a few hours what it took me three years of seminary to learn?" pastors ask.

This book is dedicated to the principle that effective Bible teaching by both professional pastors and lay people is a goal whose time has come.

PART 1

Effective Teaching

1

The Church's Unfinished Task

When we speak of effective Bible teaching as the church's unfinished task, we do not wish to minimize much that is good in how the Bible is taught and studied today. The task is already under way, and most churches have a tradition of past successes on which to build. Published Sunday school materials and inductive Bible-study guides likewise contain much that is good.

To complete the task of teaching the Bible with excellence, however, will require that we improve what currently exists. We need to look honestly at where Bible teaching stands today and diagnose where it fails. Then we must devise strategies to correct the system where it is weak. This chapter contains our analysis of those areas where Bible teaching is currently failing and how it can be strengthened.

How the Church Has Fooled Itself About Bible Teaching

One reason for the difficulty the church has in diagnosing its problems with Bible teaching is that it has been conditioned to focus on the teacher rather than on teaching. Our culture, including the Christian segment of it, is obsessed with personality cults. We therefore measure the success of Bible teaching in terms of high class interest and charismatic teaching personalities. If classes are full and students are enthusiastic, what can possibly be wrong?

The truth is that the issues are not that simple. Consider two case studies that we recall from our past experiences as Sunday school attendees.

The Class That Knew It Failed

The vacant stares were the first clue that something was not clicking. After that, the evidence continued to mount. Long years of schooling had conditioned the audience to hide its inattention. But the facade of interest was crumbling.

More and more blank expressions, yawns, whispered conversations, and pitiful looks of boredom telegraphed the message to Bob (as we will call this teacher) that he had lost his class. Like the pilot of an airplane that plummets to earth, Bob desperately tried to regain the class's attention.

He stepped forward. He raised his voice. He glanced up from the floor and scanned the class for an attentive pair of eyes. He hoped that a little variety would add the needed spark. Just for good measure, he asked a question. To his horror, the question hung awkwardly in midair before falling at his feet. No one scrambled to pick it up. He answered the question himself, as he had done so many times before, and sighed with relief when the end-of-class bell finally rang.

Bob left the classroom with a nagging feeling that he had blown it again. He had bored an entire class for an entire hour. His conversation with class members convinced him that his worst fears were correct. Not even the most polite and undiscerning among them thanked him for the lesson.

In the tranquility of a Sunday afternoon, post-teaching depression descended with a vengeance. It was painful to recall the class session. What was even worse, Bob knew that his remorse would not automatically lead to a better session next week. Sometimes class went well, and sometimes it went poorly, but he was never sure why one thing worked and another didn't.

Bob's case illustrates one of our problems: *because we focus on the teacher rather than teaching, we do not know how to diagnose our problems and strengths in Bible teaching.* Knowing that Bob is not Mr. Personality in the classroom, we assume that he cannot rise above mediocrity and do not inquire into the approach and content of his teaching. It so happens that he can be an excellent Bible teacher with proper diagnosis of his teaching.

The premise of this book is that it is possible to diagnose with precision what goes well and poorly in the classroom. It is also possible to prescribe a cure for every ailment.

The Class That Thought It Succeeded

At the very hour that Bob was struggling through his class, Mary's class in the next room was flying high. Mary (as we will call her) was an enthusiastic and witty teacher

who held her class spellbound. This multitalented teacher opened the class with a song and then proceeded to capture the audience's attention with an outlandishly amusing story from her days as a Cub Scout den mother. She proceeded to read the Scripture lesson and then generated some lively discussion by dipping selectively into some assertions made in the Sunday school quarterly.

When the discussion began to wander, Mary stepped in. The sheer charisma of her personality riveted the class's attention. She sustained their interest with another well-chosen illustration and then drafted the most unlikely assemblage of class members for a skit. The props themselves were hilarious. In a moment's time, the normally quiet banker, the clutzy salesman, and the somewhat shy pastor's wife were transformed into a drama troupe. After the laughter had subsided, Mary closed the class meeting in prayer and silently thanked God for allowing her to minister to such wonderful people.

The class was effusive in its praise. Of course people had laughed, but they were also sure that they had learned. They enjoyed their class and were exuberant about its skyrocketing attendance.

On the surface, Mary's class seems to be the opposite of Bob's. Yet for all their differences, the two classes share something in common: both are educational atrocities. In the first case, the evidence is clear and the verdict sure. The second case is more troubling because the class members are unaware of deficiencies.

Surprising as it may seem, class members are not always the best judges of educational quality. Educational research has amassed considerable evidence to show that class members can be inordinately poor at assessing the quality of their learning when a charismatic teacher is involved. In some experiments, classes have been impressed by theatrical teachers spouting off double talk or high-sounding nonsense. Charismatic teachers can seduce students into thinking they have learned when they have only been entertained.

In terms of Bible teaching, the net result in both classes is the same. Neither Bob nor Mary teaches the Bible in such a way that students encounter the text in a manner that nurtures their faith. Mary's case, then, illustrates a significant problem: *we have not learned where to look for success and failure in the teaching of the Bible.* We look too much at the teacher and not enough at the educational process and content. We assume that lively teachers whose classes are filled with enthusiastic students are effective Bible teachers. The reverse is often the case, as a survey of students' Bible knowledge would quickly reveal.

The Two Levels at Which Bible Teaching Can Fail

Autopsies of educational failures generally yield inconclusive results. A definitive answer to the question "What went wrong?" usually eludes those who probe the fading memories of a bygone class session. Occasionally a postmortem will expose such educationally defeating classroom behaviors as poor eye contact, disorganization, or confusing speech patterns. These easily identifiable behaviors range from merely annoying space fillers like "ums" to serious classroom management issues.

While these problems can markedly reduce the effectiveness of a teacher, they are also easily identified and eliminated. The problems that crippled the educational ministry of the two teachers we have cited were so big that they could be missed by someone looking for easily observable signs of ineffective teaching.

Ineffective teaching must be viewed at two levels—the *presentation level* and the *strategy/planning level*. The presentation level is actual classroom teaching. The strategy/planning level encompasses the teacher's planning and general approach to teaching, as well as decisions about the content and organization of a lesson.

The Presentation Level

Teacher-improvement books and workshops almost always focus on the presentation level. This is understandable. After all, this is the most observable level. Good communication in the classroom is like a qualifying exam: if teachers can't pass this qualification, they are not even in the running for an "effective" rating.

But by tackling problems at the presentation level, we have generally treated the symptom rather than the ailment. Presentation problems can often be solved by feedback, practice, and coaching. Often just mentioning distracting behaviors to conscientious teachers will motivate them to monitor and eliminate the tendencies.

Suppose, for example, that John is told, "That was a good presentation, John. I did notice, however, that when a hard question comes up in class you always drop your eyes and avoid eye contact with the class members. When you do this you cut yourself off from the class and from the help that class members might be able to offer on the issue." Chances are good that John's nonverbal communication can be fairly easily altered through self-monitoring.

The Strategy/Planning Level: Heart of the Matter

We are convinced that the key to better Bible teaching lies at the strategy/planning level. In fact, many presentation problems (such as stating unclear ideas, being under stress, rushing through a lesson, or confusing a class) are the result of faulty planning. Better classroom techniques will not salvage a lesson whose content was forged with flawed interpretive or educational premises at the Sunday school teacher's kitchen table on Saturday morning.

Strategy or planning problems are more difficult to spot and eliminate than are presentation problems. This should not mislead us into thinking that they do not exist. They are what lie behind many ineffective attempts at instruction and are the reason why some teachers can "do everything right" (at the presentation level) and yet be ineffective Bible teachers.

Problems at the strategy or planning level require different intervention techniques than those at the presentation level. The problems at the planning level are often missed by inexperienced observers, but the problems are real. The two teachers we described earlier failed at the strategy level. Their presentation skills were generally strong, but they lost the educational battle at the level of organization and content. Unfortunately, since their problems were not easily spotted, few people could help them reach their full potential as teachers.

Strategy and Planning Problems

Our analysis of the leading problems at the planning level is based on personal observation, conversations with students, and informal surveys we have conducted. We believe that there are seven leading culprits.

Inability to Come to Grips with a Biblical Text

The hard-working teachers described earlier had one main thing in common: they could never get a firm grip on a Bible passage. They both stared long and hard at the assigned passage. But seldom did all the pieces come together. Bob was a walking encyclopedia of facts about the Bible passage. His classroom strategy was to unload these facts on the class as he marched through the passage verse by verse.

Mary was even less able to get close to the text. In fact, she had long since given up on the possibility of getting a handle on the passages she taught. She flitted from one detail or exercise to another because she had no strategy for systematically studying a Bible passage.

When Bruce Lockerbie, dean of the faculty of Stony Brook School, was asked, "What is the problem with the way the Bible is being taught today?" he replied,

> The problem is that there's been almost no instruction in the teaching of the Bible. People who think themselves prepared to teach the Bible are often teaching *about* the Bible. In other words, they're teaching doctrinal persuasions or outlines of systematic theology.[1]

Three specific manifestations of this syndrome are especially prevalent. One is the *inability to teach a biblical passage in terms of the kind of writing it is*. Many teachers we have observed couldn't state the essential differences between a story and poem if they had to. Yet an awareness of the genre or type of writing that a passage is programs how we approach it.

To teach a psalm without realizing that poets speak a language of images and metaphors is to cut against the grain, yet this is how biblical poetry is often taught. A minister who regularly reads psalms to patients in the hospital admits that he does not choose them for Bible studies because he "can't think of anything to say about them."

Equally symptomatic of the inability to deal adequately with a biblical text is the prevailing *failure to identify the "big idea" of a biblical passage*. What we will throughout this book call "the big idea" of a passage is the thought that unifies a biblical passage and that ought to govern a class session. Ineffective teachers tend to focus on isolated facts and to present their audience with a stream of unrelated ideas in the dim hope that if they throw out enough ideas a few will stick. Research and common experience show that it does not happen that way.

Bernard Ramm once gave this humorous portrait of a

---

1. Bruce Lockerbie, interview published in *Eternity*, June 1982, p. 26.

preacher who had much to say but lacked a grasp of the passage:

> He announced his passage for the study and went to work—but what work! In his attempt to explain the text he was like a chicken with defective pecking aim. The poor hen pecks all around the corn but never hits it. She squints with her beady eye, she cocks her head, and then she pecks—and misses. She over-shoots or under-shoots. So the poor man of God does everything but explain the text. I got 30 minutes of various and divers unrelated and uninspiring pious observations. Each observation was a worthy one. But the passage itself remained untouched. We had been all around the text but never in it. Pious observations are not Bible study.[2]

This situation is extremely common, and it leads to a third symptom—*escape from the biblical text to other material.* It is easy to identify people who do not know how to interact with a biblical text in terms of the kind of writing it is. Such people talk about matters beyond the text itself—about the writer, the cultural context, and that perennial favorite, "background material." Teachers (and preachers) who do not know how to talk about the text talk about other things. They fill the time with class discussions, "creative activities," and moralizing. They share anecdotes, tell jokes, and introduce illustrations related to the subject of the passage under consideration. But they do not analyze the passage itself.

Excessive Confidence in Published Materials

Using curriculum materials can help a teacher, but that practice does not eliminate the teacher's need to arrive at a personal understanding of a passage. One of us remembers being in a particularly awful Bible study in which the

---

2. Bernard Ramm, "But It Isn't Bible Study," *Eternity*, February 1960, p. 21.

leader floundered helplessly while time dripped with painful slowness. The leader bombarded the group with a stream of isolated observations and a series of anecdotes and applications. But nothing fit together.

During the post-study chitchat, the teacher admitted that he had "used someone else's notes." He had tried to lead using someone else's preparation. Many publishers of Bible-study materials have fostered such a practice by their promise to equip any teacher to teach a passage with an hour of preparation.

Five Ways to Avoid Interpreting a Biblical Text

When teachers do not know how to come to grips with a biblical text, they find other ways to fill the time. Here are five classic ways to avoid analyzing a text in terms of the type of writing it is. As you read these pieces of commentary on the story of the separation of Abraham and Lot (Gen. 13), try to identify the common activity that each specimen represents.

Exhibit A. When the land was unable to support the flocks of both Abraham and Lot, Abraham proposed that he and Lot choose separate areas in which to live. Abraham allowed Lot to choose where he wanted to live, on the understanding that he himself would move in the other direction. Lot looked around and was attracted to the well-watered land of the Jordan valley. He chose this territory and moved to Sodom, which was known for its immorality. Abraham dwelt in the land of Canaan.

Exhibit B. In this story, Lot represents the person who lives according to the flesh. Abraham is the person who lives by the Spirit. The riches of Abraham are a picture of the riches we have in Christ when we walk in the Spirit. The land of Canaan, the promised land, represents the promised Holy Spirit. Sodom is a symbol of the flesh. Lot's choice of Sodom as a place to live is a choice to live by the flesh. The well-watered Jordan valley that tempts Lot to move there represents Satan, who lures people to live by the flesh.

Exhibit C. Verse 2 tells us that Abraham was very rich. This shows us that riches are a blessing from God. This verse about Abraham's wealth should encourage us to be diligent in our work, knowing that God wants us to be successful, just as Abraham was. God will reward our hard work, not our laziness.

Exhibit D. Verse 2 informs us that Abraham was wealthy in flocks and herds. We know that this wealth did not destroy Abraham's faith in God. This reminds us of 1 Timothy 6:17, which states, "As for the rich in this world, charge them not to be haughty, nor to set their hopes on uncertain riches but on God." Verses 8 and 9 tell us that Abraham offered Lot the opportunity to choose where he wished to live. Abraham here obeys the command in Philippians 2:4—"Let each of you look not only to his own interests, but also to the interests of others."

Exhibit E. In this chapter Abraham is a type (foreshadowing) of Christ. Abraham lived a life of self-sacrifice in order to benefit Lot. So Christ led a life of self-denial for the sake of others. Abraham lived by faith in God's promises. The Gospels portray Christ as living in the strength of the promises of his heavenly Father. Abraham was a peacemaker, just as Christ was. Abraham talked with God, just as Jesus did on many occasions. The story of Abraham thus points us to its fulfillment in the life of Christ.

Here are five ways in which, through the centuries and today, teachers and commentators have managed to create the appearance of analyzing the text while actually avoiding it. Teacher A paraphrased the passage instead of stating analytic insights. Teacher B allegorized the passage. Teacher C, assuming that every verse (rather than the passage as a whole) must yield a meaning, moralized on the individual verses. Teacher D, unable to treat the story as a story, took his students on a bicycle trip through parallel passages elsewhere in the Bible. And Teacher E, in a process of interpretation known as typology, treated the details in the story as saying something about the life and work of Christ.

Why do teachers do these things? They do not know how to come to grips with the passage as a story and as a whole, so they find substitute ways of dealing with the passage, actually avoiding the text itself.

We need to be reminded, therefore, that teachers can never teach effectively beyond their grasp of a subject. They may be able to teach beyond their own experiences, but they cannot teach what they do not understand. Merely parroting a prepared lesson is not teaching. It is just that—parroting. Someone stated it well when he noted that

"I can't teach you anything I don't know" is such an easy, silly, stupid thing to say. And yet we have to say it. If I'm going to stand in front of a group, I had better know something or have something to say to them.[3]

Personal ownership of what one teaches is the minimum requirement for effective Bible teaching.

Another reason we cannot put all our faith in curriculum writers is that they sometimes let us down. Recently some junior high material on the Old Testament prophets passed over our desk. The lesson on Jeremiah focused on both the prophet's and Jesus' use of "object lessons" in their ministries. The study concluded with an application involving the energy crisis. The more we read, the more

3. Leo F. Buscaglia, *Living, Loving and Learning* (New York: Fawcett, 1983), p. 10.

bewildered we became. The author obviously did not know what the main point of the chapter in Jeremiah was.

To compensate for this lack of understanding, the writer focused on some concrete aspects of Jeremiah's ministry and for good measure mentioned Jesus. The use of the energy crisis as the application defies explanation. Much as we may dislike admitting it, curriculum writers and Bible commentators sometimes miss the point. A teacher must be critical enough to spot such lapses. We have designed this book to help teachers gain the skill and confidence to make wise decisions about curricula and commentaries.

Too Many Facts, Not Enough Meaning

We live in an age of cheap and available information. Factual information about the Bible is readily at hand. But despite all the biblical information available, the church is often lacking in maturity and spiritual understanding, and its biblical illiteracy is often alarming.

In our information age we desperately need people who understand the big ideas of their faith and who can use these to guide their lives and the mission of the church. "Running out of information is not a problem," writes John Naisbitt, "but drowning in it is."[4]

It is our use of Bible knowledge, not the mere possession of Bible facts, that produces growth toward godliness. To know who composed the Book of Ruth or where Moab is or what a kinsman-redeemer was will not by itself direct our lives. Knowing that God's providence is at work in the daily routine will. Of course, such knowledge emerges from specific details, but an effective teacher weaves them into life-changing concepts.

Misconceptions About the Bible

To teach the Bible accurately, we need to know what we are teaching. A lot of Bible teaching is based on mis-

4. John Naisbitt, as quoted by K. Patricia Cross, *AAHE [American Association for Higher Education] Bulletin*, September 1985, p. 11.

conceptions about the book we teach. Because the Bible is our religious authority, we slip into viewing it as something that it is emphatically *not*—a theological outline with proof texts attached. "Why didn't God just give us an outline?" a new convert asked one of us. We don't know why, but he didn't.

A look at published Sunday school materials and many Bible commentaries shows how thoroughly they have reduced the Bible to a single type of material—abstract, conceptual, and theological. Consider our sermon outlines and the headings in Bible commentaries or study guides. They name theological and moral propositions

instead of the human experiences and images that actually make up the biblical text. When we label Psalm 23 as a psalm dealing with providence, we lose sight of the sheep and grass and water that make up the poem.

Somehow the rich humanity and everyday realism of the Bible get flattened into religious platitudes in much Bible teaching. The Bible emerges as a serious "spiritual" book, unlike other books in our familiar experience. "I guess I just don't know how to carry over to the Bible what I know about other books," a student recently confided regarding her inability to deal with the Psalms as poetry.

Overloading the Student

A leading hindrance to effective Bible teaching is bombarding a class with too much data. It is easy for teachers who have immersed themselves in preparation to forget that class members come to the passage without benefit of such preparation.

Overloading the student can take several forms. Well-meaning Bible teachers who want to make historical passages come to life often end up burying the learners beneath a mountain of names, dates, and places. Similarly, people desire to see their Bible heroes as real people with whom they can identify. The danger is that teachers who set out to paint a living picture end up overwhelming their students with long lists of "interesting facts."

Another complaint that we hear from adults is that teachers often give them insufficient time to adjust to a text. When using cross-references, teachers seemingly just drop people into another text. Explanations of the context and message of the parallel text, if given at all, usually come while people are busy thumbing through their Bibles trying to find the passage. To understand a biblical text takes time, and traveling between texts with breakneck speed leaves students bewildered.

Our college students tell us that the use of undefined theological terms was a major problem for them in junior high school and high school. Terms like *providence* and *justification* and *morality* were tossed at them with abandon, even though these terms had little meaning for them. The same thing can happen in adult classes.

Trying to Do Too Much in a Session

Many Bible teachers try to accomplish too much in each lesson. They would accomplish more if they set more modest and realistic goals. The educational "rule of simplicity" tells us that doing less may be a way of accomplishing more. Alfred North Whitehead once asserted, "We enunciate two educational commandments, 'Do not teach too many subjects,' and again, 'What you teach, teach thoroughly.'"[5]

It is of course legitimate to focus on several aspects of a Bible passage. But we should heed the advice of Reuel L. Howe, who listened to hundreds of sermons and solicited comments from lay people who listened to recorded sermons at his retreat center. He found himself agreeing with their biggest complaint: the sermons contained too many unrelated ideas.[6]

Ineffectiveness in Bridging the Gap

"Bridging the gap" is the term used by Bible expositors to refer to the process by which we make the biblical text relevant to modern living. Good biblical interpretation must ask and answer two questions—what a passage *meant* to the original audience and what it *means* to us today. Bridging the gap requires us to perform both activities. This is exactly what is often missing. Despite our affirmation that the Bible is our rule of faith and practice, many Christians read it with a disquieting sense that its shepherds, kings, and battles have little to do with modern life.

Several signs tell us when the gap is not being bridged. One is uninterpreted biblical material. We are talking here about the Sunday school lesson filled with biblical facts that are treated as an end in themselves. This has long characterized curriculum materials for children. Instead of interpreting a Bible passage, teachers often simply paraphrase its content in their own words.

Teachers who fail to interpret biblical material sometimes take a one-way journey to the world of the Bible. This was teacher Bob's practice. He was great at telling

5. Alfred North Whitehead, *The Aims of Education* (New York: Macmillan, 1929, 1967), p. 2.

6. Reuel L. Howe, *Partners in Preaching: Clergy and Laity in Dialogue* (New York: Seabury, 1967), p. 26.

his classes all they could ever want to know about the world of a Bible passage. But he rarely made the return trip from the world of the Bible to our own world.

Another thing that signals inadequate bridging of the gap is insufficient application of biblical principles to a student's life. "What difference is this supposed to make in my life this week?" is the question often left unanswered in contemporary Bible teaching. In fact, we have almost come to expect it. When we speak of someone's being "a good Bible teacher," we usually mean that he or she is full of facts about the Bible but may make little attempt to wrestle with applying those facts to modern living.

Another failure to bridge the gap is neglecting to make the journey from our time and place to the world of the Bible. Teacher Mary, for example, stayed rooted firmly in twentieth-century America. She made no pretense of living inside the world of the biblical text. She was an enthusiast for "relevance," and her lessons were in a sense *all* application.

In addition to these ways of neglecting to bridge the gap, there are wrong ways of doing it. One is the old standby of moralizing about isolated details in a text instead of first mastering the passage as a whole and then deducing principles from it. In the story of David and Goliath, for example, we read that "David left his things with the keeper of supplies, ran to the battle lines and greeted his brothers" (1 Sam. 17:22 NIV). A Bible lesson entitled "Be a Giant-Killer" moralizes thus: "A giant-killer does not carry excess baggage—nonessential things and petty personal preferences—into battle."

Closely related is the persistent syndrome of allegorizing or spiritualizing a biblical passage. One of us recalls a teacher of an adult class who did a good job of treating the surface details in a battle story in the Book of Joshua and then admitted that he didn't know how the story applied to our lives today. A class member came to the rescue by asking, "Why can't we spiritualize the story?" The suggestion made a big hit, and in no time at all the story had been allegorized to "teach" such far-flung truths as Christ's atonement and the Holy Spirit's infilling. The impulse to allegorize is one of the most pervasive features of Bible teaching in our day.

Keys to Improved Teaching

If we have correctly diagnosed the problems in contemporary Bible teaching, the solutions to the problems can be identified with equal precision. The following list outlines our proposed solutions. We treat them briefly because they are a virtual outline of the entire book that follows. Most of these points will receive chapter-length treatment later in the book.

Focusing on the Bible Itself

Bible teaching should be just that—*Bible* teaching. We are convinced that people avoid the text because they do not know how to interact with it. We are also confident that the tools of textual analysis can be learned by any committed teacher.

Chief among the tools of textual analysis is approaching a biblical text in terms of the kind of writing it is. The technical term for type of writing is *genre*. In defending genre study, C. S. Lewis said that "the first qualification for judging any piece of workmanship from a corkscrew to a cathedral is know *what* it is—what it was intended to do and how it is meant to be used."[7] Applied to the Bible, this means that stories must be taught as stories, poems as poems, and theological exposition as theological exposition.

When we approach the Bible in terms of its genres, it will quickly become evident how much of the Bible is

7. C. S. Lewis, *A Preface to Paradise Lost* (New York: Oxford University Press, 1942), p. 1.

literary (though not fictional) in nature. It is filled with stories, poems, visions, proverbs, letters, and other literary forms. That is why (to quote Lewis again) there is a "sense in which the Bible, since it is after all literature, cannot properly be read except as literature; and the different parts of it as the different sorts of literature they are."[8]

Teaching the Big Idea

The antidote to the "too many ideas" about which the sermon listeners complained is to make sure that a Bible lesson unifies all the details around a single focus. We are so sure that this is a major factor that determines whether a lesson is good or bad that it will be a unifying theme of this book. People will "get the point" only if the lesson has one.

From time immemorial, three time-honored principles have been said to govern a good essay or speech: unity, coherence, and emphasis. These same principles apply to a good Bible study. When applied, they produce the clarity of thought that characterizes any good learning experience. By clarity we mean more than clear ideas. We also mean that a lesson has a goal in view toward which the teacher moves the class. Such goal-centered lessons will of course avoid the abuse of overloading students and trying to do too much in a given class session.

Using Our Imagination

In keeping with the kind of book the Bible is, teaching can be significantly strengthened by more reliance on the imagination. The imagination is our image-making and image-perceiving capacity. Given this definition, the Bible is a predominantly imaginative book. It is filled with the experiences and images of real life. When asked to define *neighbor*, Jesus told a story.

---

8. C. S. Lewis, *Reflections on the Psalms* (New York: Harcourt, Brace and World, 1958), p. 3.

"The Lord is my shepherd," the psalmist tells us, but much Bible teaching assumes that in discussing Psalm 23 we should talk about more "spiritual" things than sheep and grass. Bible teaching needs to do justice to the experiential and literary nature of the Bible itself. In the terms popularized by contemporary psychology, Bible teaching needs more appeals to the right side of the brain, which thinks in images. This, too, will be a leading theme of this book.

This, in turn, relates to the point we made about teaching based on inaccurate views of the Bible. If the Bible is not a theology outline with proof texts attached, we will obviously miss the boat if we treat it that way. The content of the Bible is much closer to lived experience than many theological treatments of it would suggest. A leading ally in making the Bible seem relevant and accessible to people is the ability to apply to the Bible what we know about other books that we read and about our experiences of life.

Interpreting the Meaning of Bible Passages

It is impossible to teach the Bible well without interpreting it. The facts do not always speak for themselves. Yet it is this very process of moving from text to meaning that baffles most people. The reason some teachers leave biblical details uninterpreted and others allegorize them is that they do not know what else to do.

We spoke earlier about the syndrome of "too many facts, not enough meaning." The way out of the maze is to reach a high enough point that we can see the overall pattern of a Bible passage and the big ideas of the Christian faith based on the Bible. Interpretation is simply another word for this process of reaching the vantage point from which to see the big picture.

Interpretation is not a mystical process. It is governed by long-established principles. We discuss these principles of interpretation in the chapters that follow. They are the skills that can be mastered by any lay person who possesses the desire and gifts to teach.

Bridging the Gap

Our entire approach to Bible teaching in this book is based on the model of a two-way journey from our world to the biblical passage and then back to our own world. We will call this "bridging the gap." It is a mindset that can be fostered. With imagination and creativity, we can learn to see ourselves and our world in the stories of the Bible. We can learn to state details from the Bible in contemporary terms and counterparts. The Samaritan woman whom Jesus met at the well, for example, had been divorced five times and currently had a live-in boyfriend.

Bible teachers also need to develop the knack for seeing recognizable human experience in a biblical text. Such experience exists at multiple levels—physical, emotional, moral, and psychological. When David asserts that before he confessed his sin his "body wasted away, . . . for day and night [God's] hand was heavy" upon him, he is talking about such recognizable experiences as insomnia, loss of appetite, psychosomatic ailments, guilt-related stress, and emotional fatigue.

In much Bible teaching today, the biblical text and the world in which we live are both mentioned, but they rarely touch each other, except perhaps at the beginning and end of the lesson. Such teaching resembles a rail fence in which the boards run parallel but meet only at an occasional post. What we need is Bible teaching that resembles a picket fence, with the biblical world and our own experiences joined at many points.

Why the Problems of Bible Teaching Must Be Addressed

Putting the Bible in the hands of the laity stands as one of the much-heralded fruits of the Protestant Reformation. No longer the exclusive property of the ordained clergy, the Bible was set free and made available to all Christians. Luther himself translated the Bible into his native German, and other Reformers showed equal concern that the Bible be made available in the vernacular.

Today the Protestant laity possess the Bible in staggering numbers and multitudinous versions. But when measured by how these Bibles are actually used, many churches have failed to meet the ideals of the Reformation. The Protestant tradition has been quicker to assert the right and responsibility of Bible study in both the home and the church than it has been to equip the laity for this task.

> Perhaps it has not fully dawned on the preachers of our time that preaching needs to be preceded by strong programs of teaching. The preacher's words fall on barren ground where the people have not first been taught *how* to hear afresh the good news! How to listen, how to weigh and evaluate, how to interpret the lines of Scripture that appear in the sermon—all these "how to's" are the product of careful preparation, of *teaching*.
>
> Locke Bowman, *Teaching Today: The Church's First Ministry* (Philadelphia: Westminster, 1980), pp. 86–87.

Pastors typically exhort their parishioners to read and study the Bible and are distressed when the advice goes unheeded. But seldom do ministers provide their congregations or even their Sunday school teachers with a method for reading, studying, and teaching the Bible. A number of factors promote this odd situation.

Many pastors have been trained to study the Bible from an academic perspective. In seminary they studied biblical languages and devoted considerable energy to learning the technical tools of biblical interpretation. Consequently, many pastors do not know how someone lacking biblical languages and technical exegetical skills can be trained to interpret the Bible well. Furthermore, many pastors fear that lay Bible study, especially in small groups, will lead to far-out interpretations and theological chaos in the church.

Pastors also know all too well how complex the task of interpreting and teaching the Bible has become as a result of modern biblical scholarship. Biblical languages, archaeological finds, geography, and textual studies can all enlighten the biblical text. But while enlightening, they vastly complicate the process of interpretation. Though pastors would be hesitant to admit it, they tend to operate on the premise that biblical interpretation should be left to the professionals. Consequently they work hard on their sermons in order to open the dark and mysterious Scriptures to the ordinary Christian.

> The minister who refuses to come down from his pulpit and participate in the work of teaching is like a farmer who scatters seed on the land and refuses to do anything more until the harvest. In fact, if he withholds himself from the more open and vulnerable situation of the teacher, he is likely to lack the intimate knowledge of what is happening in his people's lives which alone makes it possible for him to be an effective harvester. The ministry of the Word is a ministry to people, not in the mass but as individuals, to be exercised with loving care.
>
> James D. Smart, *The Teaching Ministry of the Church* (Philadelphia: Westminster, 1954), pp. 22–23.

The Protestant tradition of Bible translation and of commitment to the ideal of the priesthood of all believers has placed effective Bible teaching on the agenda of the church. Good teaching, in turn, requires training and practice. Teachers can learn by doing and by reflecting on what they have done.

Teacher training should receive a much higher priority in the church than it typically does. With it, teachers can learn to master a biblical text in terms of the kind of writing it is, to interpret its meaning, and to show the relevance of the Bible to everyday living. It is time to complete the church's unfinished task.

2

The Tasks of
the Effective Teacher

Teachers are the single most important ingredient in any educational program. To be sure, curriculum, classrooms, and equipment are significant factors. But ultimately it is the teacher who opens the door to high-quality instruction.

It is unfortunate, therefore, that churches devote more careful thought to buying a new printer or choosing the color of carpeting than they do to selecting the next quarter's Sunday school teachers. Too often they recruit teachers on the basis of their availability, personality, or out-of-classroom behavior. Such a teacher selection process makes as much sense as choosing a vacuum cleaner "because it looks nice."

Would we choose a car mechanic because he has an outgoing personality? Do we select a doctor on the basis of attractive appearance? Why, then, are personality and style often the main criteria by which we choose our Bible teachers?

Effective teachers are distinguished from their less effective peers chiefly by what they do *in the classroom*. This may seem obvious, but it is often overlooked. We all know people who are recruited to teach because of their

"bright personality," who really know the Bible, are godly models, love children, or are fun to be around.

These are all positive characteristics, but they may have little to do with what the teacher actually does in the classroom. None of us would select a surgeon simply because he has a warm personality or wears fashionable clothes. We would want some assurance that he or she is competent in the operating room. We should judge Bible teachers by their success in terms of how much their students learn and apply from the Bible. In the remainder of this chapter we will describe those things that effective teachers do in their classes.

Fostering Active Learning

Our assumption that learners must be actively involved in their education shapes our entire approach to teaching in this book. When we speak of active learning, we do not mean outward activity. Students may be actively learning in a lecture class where they never say a word. These same students may be busy talking in a discussion-oriented class, yet be so minimally challenged that despite all the talk and discussion they become passive.

Active learning describes educational experiences that engage students and prompt them to wrestle with information, test its validity, find ways of using what is learned, and relate or adapt it to previously learned material. The biggest single mistake made by educators who wish to promote active learning is to confuse it with mere activity.

What, then, constitutes active learning? Active learning happens when teachers achieve the classroom conditions that we outline in this chapter. Although teachers cannot learn for students, they can promote the conditions under which learning will flourish.

Motivating Students

Motivation in learning is based on a very simple educational axiom: *unless people are excited to learn something, their learning will be superficial and short-lived.* Because of the power of motivation to transform the ordinary student into a stellar achiever, it has an almost magical quality. Of course teachers cannot reach inside students and flip a switch that turns on an energizing source of motivation. Yet effective teachers do things that motivate students to learn.

One of us recalls a college pastor who did a wonderful job of convincing new Christians that despite their past they could learn to live with Christ as their Lord. His sincere belief that people could change provided the impetus for change in people who had heard few encouraging words about themselves. Teachers can motivate students by showing that goals are attainable.

Teachers can also motivate students through affirmation. It is a myth that teachers who carry a big club motivate students, while affirming and positive teachers produce sluggards. Educational research shows that the reverse is usually true.

Teachers who do a good job of motivation also convey the impression that they believe what they are teaching is of momentous importance. They communicate this belief nonverbally by preparing well and by showing excitement for the material. (A particularly effective way to kill student interest in a text is to explain that you found it tedious, technical, and hard to follow.) Teachers can communicate their love for the subject by telling students how much they enjoy it, or how it affects their lives. One of us was deeply influenced to read the Bible by a college pastor who, in the midst of his excellent presentations, included "asides" about how vital the devotional reading of Scripture was to him.

Christian educators are particularly prone to assume that the importance of what they are teaching is plain for all to see. But this is to assume too much of most classes. That is why there is a bit of the salesperson in good teachers. They take time to package and market their material and sell their students on the importance of what they are teaching. In short, if you want to motivate your students, show them that the material is meaningful.

We must never forget that all true education is self-education. No teacher can make students learn, a fact that is ignored by contemporary approaches to education that pamper students and ask teachers to shoulder the entire responsibility for education.

Teachers can never take full credit when their students excel, nor should they heap all the blame on themselves when their students fail to master the material. Teachers must teach effectively and in the process foster active learning, but they have neither the responsibility nor the means to take over the personalities of students and make them learn. Unlike indoctrination or brainwashing, education requires the student to comprehend, accept, and act on what is taught.

Teaching can be no more than guiding of the activity of the pupil. It is impossible for a teacher to transfer knowledge from a book, or from any other source, to the learner's mind. No one can communicate facts, ideas, principles, skills, attitudes, or ideals to another person. A teacher can give a pupil nothing; the pupil must take whatever he gets. The learner is not a vessel to receive what is poured into it nor is he an inert mass of something to be moulded by the application of external pressure. Instead, he is a living being whose growth is to be directed by the teacher. All learning comes through self-activity; the task of teaching is the task of stimulating, guiding, and directing the activity of the learner.

C. B. Eavey, *Principles of Teaching for Christian Teachers* (Grand Rapids: Zondervan, 1940, 1968), p. 159.

For this reason, education will never be 100 percent successful. Self-willed individuals will often reject what is taught. Learners may not be motivated enough to spend the time and effort required to master a subject. There will always be indifferent students.

An old educational question asks, "Has a teacher taught if the students have not learned?" Student-centered educators will shout an emphatic NO because they think that it is the teacher's job to insure that students learn. We disagree. All that teachers can do is *help* students learn.

Teachers in our day have burdened themselves with a lot of false guilt, partly because people are often indifferent and mentally lazy today. We need to remind each other, therefore, that teachers can never do for students what they are unwilling to do for themselves.

Practical Suggestions

Let students see that you are taking the time to prepare the lessons carefully. Of course it is best if they see this from the depth of your preparation, rather than from your tales of hours spent slaving over the lesson materials.

Place an emphasis on comprehension rather than simple recall of facts. Ask your class questions to check their understanding and see that they know more than just "the right words."

Think of ways to sell the course material to your students. Take time to package it and market it so that the learners can see that it is important and appealing. Make an effort to give the students a reason for wanting to learn the material you offer.

Small-group activities are effective in activating students to learn. Such activities are based on the educational axiom that students can learn from each other as well as from the teacher. An effective strategy is therefore to assign topics for groups of two to five people to discuss.

Another tried-and-true technique is the case study. Here the teacher poses a real-life situation. If possible, it should be posed as an actual problem that needs to be solved. In effect, the teacher gives the class a true story without an ending. Ask the class or individual groups to solve the problem in light of the lesson.

Clarity of Communication

Anyone who has spent time back-packing knows what a difference the condition of the trail can make. A rocky and root-covered trail forces hikers to focus almost all of their concentration on not falling. Similarly, unclear communication patterns require the student to expend considerable sums of energy simply to receive and decode what is being said. Learners may have to concentrate so much on following what is being said that they will have little opportunity to reflect on what they hear.

One of the rules of clarity is simplicity. Knowing too much about a subject, or having too detailed and precise a grasp of a Bible passage, can actually hamper a teacher. Teachers who know less about a subject often communicate more clearly than those who know more. We are not advocating meager knowledge of a subject but rather a crucial rule of teaching: *be willing to streamline (leave some material out) for the sake of clarity.*

> Knowing material well is quite different from being able to present it clearly, however. Knowledge is far more than the accumulation of isolated facts and figures. It involves a deeper understanding, an ability to "walk around" facts and see them from different angles.
>
> Joseph Lowman, *Mastering the Techniques of Teaching* (San Francisco: Jossey-Bass, 1984), p. 10.

Effective teachers have learned to travel slowly. They know that they often teach more by teaching less. This does not mean traveling through books of the Bible at a snail's pace or extracting twenty lessons from a chapter of the Bible. Instead it involves acknowledging that a stream of unrelated or marginally related ideas soon wearies a listener. Good teachers know what is important and make the important ideas clear to their students. They are also willing to exploit the "teachable moments" that arise in a class. And of course they are eager to pause and explain material to students.

Practical Suggestions

Avoid undefined technical terms. One of the leading complaints about Bible teaching that we uncovered in an informal poll was being turned off by teachers who used undefined terms.

Be redundant. The sage advice of "tell them what you are going to say, say it, and summarize what you said" is effective.

Give people re-entry points. A good lesson should encourage people to make connections between the lesson and life. Thus even the best teacher will "lose" students for a moment as they ponder what they are learning. Fill your lesson with appropriate pauses and summaries so that class members who have gotten sidetracked can come back in. Prominent outlines, such as those on a chalkboard or overhead projector, can also help people tune back in to a lesson.

Think visually as a teacher. Write key words and lists on a chalkboard or use an overhead projector to accomplish the same effect. The benefits of this are several: such lists keep a student's attention focused on the topic being discussed; they insure that the teacher does not move too fast from one idea to the next; and they can be a good way of allowing a class to contribute to an ongoing discovery of truth about a topic.

Challenging Students

"He teaches and asks questions so that you think you'll just die unless you figure out the answer." This is how a college student described her "best Bible teacher." She praised his wit and clarity, but said his real forte was asking questions that stimulated the class to think. This master teacher had figured out a way of challenging learners without unsettling their faith. He teased them into thought. He caused them to sit up and think about the implications of what they were learning.

This teacher played a valuable role in the lives of his students by challenging their hand-me-down faith and helping them construct a Christ-centered faith of their own. Not every teacher can or should be a challenger. Some teachers make their impact on students by their support and encouragement, but the challenging and controversial teachers are some of the best at fostering active learning.

Practical Suggestions

Use case studies. Find a real-life but hard-to-solve problem from your own experience, or one reported in the media, and ask your class to solve it. Have them address the case from the perspective of what they're learning. Challenge answers until the students have wrestled with both the case and material being studied. Do not try to force the class to reach a consensus.

Also use pithy quotations. Find a catchy saying that goes along with the lesson. Have people respond to the quotation: How good a summary is it? What does it overlook? How would you change it?

As a variation on the technique of using quotations, ask the class what headline they would give to the material being studied if they were presenting a biblical passage in the form of a newspaper account.

Do not be too quick to settle controversy when it arises in a class.

Making the Class Minutes Count

One of the popular research findings of the 1970s was dubbed "time on task." This research found that students' learning was significantly related to the amount of time they spent engaged in learning a subject. These research findings delivered a clear message: students learn what they spend time on.

Let's apply the principle to a class that violated it. Once upon a time there was a Sunday school class that wanted to do everything. They wanted a class that was warm and supportive, that prayed for each other, that heard good Bible teaching, and that had fun together. To meet these goals, they divided their hour into the following pieces.

First, the class usually began fifteen minutes late because the first worship service always went "just a little over." The group devoted ten minutes to coffee and doughnuts, followed by about ten minutes of sharing. This gave the Bible teacher fifteen to twenty minutes before prayer time. Needless to say, in their well-intentioned desire to do everything, the class did far less than they had planned.

Unless the time for Bible teaching is protected from inroads, so-called Bible studies become something else—sharing groups, fellowship groups, prayer groups, but emphatically not Bible studies.

Practical Suggestions

Be realistic in your expectations of what a class can accomplish. It is impossible to do more than one or two things thoroughly in an hour. If it is the purpose of a group to study the Bible, other activities will have to be eliminated or curtailed.

If the goal of the class is to study the Bible but members also wish to socialize, schedule out-of-class times for social activities.

Even time spent in classroom instruction needs to be protected from digressions. The opening moments of class sessions are notoriously inefficient. Begin on time and move directly to the important business of teaching. Avoid a time-filling "ten-minute review" of the previous lesson. Stick to the subject and avoid riding hobby horses.

If you habitually slight the actual Bible teaching that goes on during a class session, either tape a class meeting and analyze where the time went or ask a class member to keep track of how every minute was spent.

Focusing on the Big Idea

Along with not knowing how to come to grips with a biblical passage, the biggest cause for failure in Bible teaching is lack of focus. One of the fallacies abroad among teachers and preachers of the Bible is the assumption that if a Bible study or sermon deals with a single biblical passage it will automatically be unified. But in order to be unified, a sermon or Bible study needs a thesis—a statement of what the passage is about and what it asserts regarding that subject.

Someone who listened to hundreds of taped sermons and held discussions with lay people concluded that the commonest complaint about sermons is that they contain "too many ideas."[1] Did these people want shorter sermons? Probably not. Their complaint was that sermons contained too many separate ideas that were not related to an overriding framework. The same thing is true of many Bible studies.

One of us recalls a Sunday school teacher who described his method of preparation thus: "I just read through the passage and see what sparks me." The resulting lesson was a string of miscellaneous observations and moralizings, not a unified whole. No wonder he professed to "like long passages," and no wonder his classes were overwhelmed with the quantity of isolated facts that he presented.

The antidote to the problem is simple, though mastering it takes some practice. It consists of writing down a statement of topic and theme for every Bible passage that one teaches and then slanting the entire lesson around that "big idea." The topic is what the passage is about. The theme is what the passage says *about* that subject. This procedure is so important that we will devote an entire chapter to it later in this book.

1. Reuel L. Howe, *Partners in Preaching: Clergy and Laity in Dialogue* (New York: Seabury, 1967), p. 26.

How important is it to identify the big idea of a biblical passage? We found out in a course that we offer in teaching the Bible. Part of the course consists of students leading inductive Bible studies. A common complaint during the first year was boredom during the Bible studies. After we required leaders to write out a statement of topic and theme, the complaints about boredom simply ceased.

> Perhaps the most basic thing that can be said about human memory, after a century of intensive research, is that unless a detail is placed into a structured pattern, it is rapidly forgotten. Detailed material is conserved in memory by the use of simplified ways of representing it.
>
> Jerome S. Bruner, *The Process of Education* (Cambridge: Harvard University Press, 1977), p. 24.

How can formulating a specific thesis about a biblical passage make that much difference? It insures that the lesson will have a single focus and that the class will have a "box" into which to put the individual points that are made during the class meeting.

Making the Truth Personal

Teaching the Bible involves far more than simply giving out information about the Bible. Bible teaching is ministering to people, liberating them from their inadequate concepts of God, expanding their notion of what it means to live faithfully before God, helping them cast aside old self-defeating habits and replace them with habits of holiness. Because teaching the Bible is ultimately ministering to people, it is important that we strive to foster classes that are supportive.

The transformational goal of Bible teaching requires an atmosphere permeated by love, acceptance, vulnerability, and genuine caring. We tend to teach the way we were taught. Since our school experiences seldom contained the type of support and personal involvement on the part of the teacher that we are talking about here, we tend to take few steps to encourage it. Yet it is a necessity, not a luxury.

If teachers see their role as simply giving out information, then of course taking time to build a supportive class atmosphere will seem extraneous to the task at hand. But *how* the Bible is taught is as important as what is taught. For the Christian teacher, instruction always becomes a sharing of one's self. Theology is more than words and ideas: it is something that a teacher must live.

The early Puritans were particularly insightful on this point. One of them defined theology as "the doctrine of living for God,"[2] thereby showing the practical nature of Christian doctrine and removing it from the realm of intellectual abstraction in which we so often place it. Another Puritan said that Christians must "speak by lives as well as words; you must live religion, as well as talk religion."[3] For the teacher, theology and Bible knowledge must be a personal experience that is shared, not simply a set of facts or ideas. This requires that teachers allow their classes to get to know them well enough that students can see what God's grace has done in their teacher's life.

The personal touch in teaching is something that can be fostered. A teacher need not be an extrovert to be a caring teacher. High-powered performances are not a requirement and can, in fact, create an impersonal atmosphere. We remember one likable teacher who was "all facts" in the classroom, but who displayed a remarkable sensitivity to others in informal settings. With the help of a friend, he was able to bring more and more of his

2. This is the famous opening sentence of William Ames's *Marrow of Theology*.

3. Eleazar Mather, *A Serious Exhortation to the Present and Succeeding Generation in New England*, as quoted by Edmund Morgan, *The Puritan Family* (New York: Harper and Row, 1966), p. 102.

interpersonal skills into the classroom. Too often intro-verted teachers see the extroverted dynamo at work and wrongly conclude that they will just have to stick with the facts.

Practical Suggestions

Ask yourself, "What do people like about me?" Then find ways to highlight these aspects of your personality in class sessions.

After completing a lesson's preparation, ponder what you can share from your own life regarding the topic. By "your own life" we mean *your* life, not first of all the life of a family member or friend.

When discussing Bible passages, point out their experiential dimension. If you show that you are attuned to ordinary human experience, your students will feel a bond with you.

Similarly, if you devote some creative thought to how a biblical passage or truth applies to everyday life, people will know that you are concerned with living the Christian truth, not simply knowing it with head knowledge.

Building a Constructive Class Atmosphere

Good teaching methods and solid lesson content do not guarantee good learning. Effective learning also requires a class atmosphere that is conducive to the interest and personal growth of students. We might call this *a constructive class atmosphere* or *a growth-producing climate*.

Many classes have impediments to a growth-producing climate. In well-established classes and Bible studies, these roadblocks may be difficult for a teacher to spot. A good starting point is to ask, "What and who does *not* contribute to a constructive climate?" One can take a careful look at this and seek to minimize the negative effects. We encourage teachers not to fix too much blame on factors outside their control, such as meeting room, class size, or group members. While these are important, teachers need to focus on what they can *do*, not on what could possibly *be*.

The key figure in establishing an open and supportive classroom atmosphere is the teacher. Teachers must be willing to be transparent. We have no interest in vulnerability for vulnerability's sake. Our self-disclosure must be purposeful and appropriate. The teacher who expects openness on the part of a class but remains a closed book will rightly be perceived as manipulative.

Humor works well at relaxing a class and preparing the way for more openness and support. The teacher's willingness to laugh at himself or herself conveys a welcome humanness. Teachers should seek to identify with the class and be open enough to allow the class to identify with them.

Teachers who are best at creating a positive classroom atmosphere know how to involve class members. If teachers can foster a sense of class "ownership," students will rise to the occasion. Often this is done through the formal means of electing officers. These officers take charge of the social and ministry aspects of the class. We have seen them both function well and falter, but ultimately what really matters is the class's perception of its role. The class needs to be encouraged to take an active role in shaping its direction and spirit. Those members with gifts in areas like hospitality and exhortation should be encouraged in their work.

Practical Suggestions

Make an effort to respond positively to appropriate self-disclosure by class members. Listen carefully to what they say and avoid "force fitting" their remarks into the lesson.

Take advantage of "teachable moments." From time to time, needs and issues will be felt as urgencies by class members. At such times the wise and sensitive teacher may set aside the lesson in favor of looking at this keenly felt topic.

Do not be too quick to offer easy solutions. When adults mention their frustrations or defeats in a class, they are seeking empathy rather than pat answers. Quick and easy answers often cut off class members who may have wise advice to offer from their personal experiences.

Maintain a creative tension between keeping the class on schedule with the content of the lesson and the need to develop personal relationships among class members (and between yourself and the class). A class session must of course provide liberating knowledge. But personal relations are also important. A responsive and vibrant atmosphere fosters good learning. You do not have to choose between solid class content and warm personal relations among class members—you need both.

Distinguishing Between Major and Minor Issues

Effective teachers know what is important in a subject. They stress what is important and cover enough ground to help students see the main thrust of a lesson or Bible passage. They also know how to provide clear pathways through a subject and avoid an excess of details.

It is exactly at these points that inexperienced or ineffective teachers are most likely to fail. Beginning teachers are notorious for trying to teach all they know in the first four weeks. They are usually overprepared for a lesson, which by itself is not a bad strategy. After all, one never knows *exactly* how long one's material will take in class.

But inexperienced teachers often fail to arrange the material into categories of primary and secondary importance. They begin at the beginning of their material, and when the bell rings they find that they have spent most of their time on background or "approach" material instead of the central point.

Pacing is also important. Students learn better if they do not feel rushed. One of the commonest failings of teachers is trying to cover too much territory in a given lesson. The effect has been compared to trying to drink from a fire hydrant. Teachers typically find it painful to omit good material from a lesson, but the important principle to follow is that less can be more and more can be less when it comes to meaningful learning.

Practical Suggestions

> Cover essential material first and leave the secondary material for last, where it can be dropped if time runs out. You need to do such planning *before* class time. Experienced teachers step into a classroom knowing what they will do and what they will omit if time starts to run short.

> The spoken word has a short life. People also find it easier to concentrate on something visual or written. It is impossible to overstate the need for a teacher to put the main concepts of a lesson in written and visual form—outlines on handouts, key phrases written on a chalkboard, overhead transparencies, and so forth. These of course take time, both in preparation and class time, but they pay big dividends. *Not* doing them is almost a ticket to ineffectiveness.

> Good teachers have learned to teach what is important and not just what they like. They have the ability to set aside pet subjects and interesting insights in favor of that which will really help students.

The Ideal Teacher

All teachers carry around in their minds a picture of the perfect teacher. Most teachers consciously and unconsciously try to fit the picture that they have of what a teacher should be. The biggest influence in our private pictures of the ideal teacher is our own past experiences—good and bad—as students sitting under teachers. But our pictures of the ideal teacher can also be influenced by metaphors that we use to describe such a teacher.

We think the ideal teacher is a guide. This metaphor reminds us in the first place that Bible teaching is a journey. It is more than a brief sprint. It involves marathon-like dedication on the part of the teacher and the student.

The image of the teacher as guide also sums up the characteristics of the effective teacher that we have suggested in this chapter. In the first place, a good travel guide is an *expert*. Guides possess a knowledge of the territory and the problems of the journey that comes through personal experience and diligent study. The very competence and superior knowledge of the guide are reassuring to travelers.

Travel guides plan a trip beforehand. They know where the group is going and make adjustments for the group as necessary. They also dispense helpful information as the group travels through an area, pointing out important details, supplying background information, and interpreting what the group is looking at. In all of these activities, we can see a correspondence between a travel guide and a good Bible teacher.

In the second place, a travel guide is a *fellow participant*. Guides know more about the territory beforehand, but they accompany the travelers on the trip. Guides and travelers look at things together. They experience the joys and hardships of the journey together. They share insights about the details of the journey. Sometimes the tables are turned and the traveler is able to offer support to the guide. In these ways, too, we can see how a good Bible teacher is like a travel guide.

Under most circumstances, a travel guide is also an *instructor*. On the first day of a tour, guides can be expected to look after members of a group and almost protect them from themselves. But gradually guides expect group members to be able to look after themselves. Without intending to do so, travelers become experts themselves. If they had to make the trip again, they could do so, and they might even be able to lead others. Travel guides can make the trip easier, but they cannot do the traveling for someone else. Similarly, teachers cannot learn for their students.

Part of the responsibility of a travel guide is to insure good *personal relationships* within the traveling community. Guides interact with group members as well as with the places that they are visiting together. They may arrange social occasions. They mingle with the group and avoid appearing standoffish. They inquire whether people's needs are being met and are prepared to get an injured traveler to the doctor if the need arises.

Finally, good guides view themselves as *servants*. It is their calling and perhaps even their full-time job to arrange trips for people, and they may use their position as a way of seeing some places that they would otherwise never visit. But they are not self-seeking people. They bear the burden of seeing to it that other people achieve their goals in traveling.

Who is the ideal teacher? He or she is a travel guide through the Bible, traveling with students through life, accompanying them with the Word through their journey and becoming a friend in the process.

3

The Teacher: The Human Element in Teaching

In our opening chapter we attributed a large share of current problems in Bible teaching to a tendency to focus on the personality of the teacher rather than the process of teaching. We do not mean to imply by this, however, that we think that the teacher is unimportant. Our concern is simply that effective teaching must be measured in terms of how successfully a teacher performs the task of teaching, and not by other considerations.

Our focus in this chapter will be on the teacher as the human element in effective Bible teaching. Not everyone feels comfortable with this human element. After all, this is what makes teaching variable and unpredictable. Some publishers of curriculum materials have responded by trying to make their materials "teacher proof." They attempt to make their instructions and resources so systematic and detailed that anyone can teach the class. In an attempt to remove the possibility of teacher error, these materials strive to eliminate the human element from teaching. Since "teacher proofing" focuses on avoiding disasters, it tends to foster mediocre rather than creative and stimulating teaching.

Dehumanizing education is not the solution to the problem of the human element in teaching. Education is a people-oriented activity. We should not try to excise the human element from teaching. Instead we should celebrate the fact that teaching is human and life-related.

Teachers, not printed curriculum materials, fine-tuned programs, or media extravaganzas, are the backbone of any good Christian education program. We need to cultivate and commend the teachers who choose to help in the teaching ministry of the church. They can have bad moments as well as good ones, but in the final analysis it is they, and not church programs, who perform the work of teaching the Bible and influencing people in their Christian growth.

The purpose of the sections that follow is to define some of the ingredients that make up the complex, unpredictable creature that we know as the teacher. As we pursue that discussion, we will see that the teacher has the potential for either good or bad influence, and is a person with his or her own passions or preoccupations relative to the task of teaching. We will also delineate the life cycle of the teacher as teacher—a life cycle that can run the gamut from the (sometimes naive) zest that accompanies accepting a teaching assignment to the discouragement and exhaustion that can afflict even the best of teachers.

The Teacher as a Means of Grace

When the apostle Paul wrote to the young and struggling pastor Timothy, he urged him to follow his example of "sound teaching" (2 Tim. 1:13 NIV). This is more than a command not to stray from doctrinal truth. John R. W. Stott reminds us that "sound" words are "healthy" words, and that the Greek expression is also used in the

Gospels for people whom Jesus had healed.[1] Good Christian teaching is healthful teaching. It is whole and complete, not diseased or maimed or lacking in essentials. The ideal that guides Christian teachers is to provide students with words that heal and restore.

In speaking such words, teachers are in the position of mediators. They stand between the Word of God and the lives of their students. In many cases they provide the very impetus for people to encounter the Bible. In the process of that encounter, they often interpret and translate the biblical text for people. With our democratic assumptions, we tend to be skeptical of the Reformers' claims that the preacher or teacher speaks the very Word of God. Yet upon reflection we can scarcely avoid the conclusion that nothing less than this is the Bible teacher's goal.

To view the teacher as the very spokesperson of God implies that God delights to work through people. Scripture and the sacraments have a powerful effect on lives, but often people are the means by which God's healing and restoring grace reaches human lives. Richard F. Lovelace has expressed it well:

> *Among the most vital means of grace are other Christians.* Neither the Bible nor the sacraments will leave the shelf or the sanctuary to rescue a Christian who is too discouraged or backslidden to pray or worship. But a concerned brother or sister will do this again and again![2]

We need to protect the human element in Bible teaching and Christian education programs. When teachers are replaced by workbooks and media and well-oiled church programs, we have done more than simply remove the unpredictable human element. We have also removed

1. John R. W. Stott, *Guard the Gospel* (Downers Grove: Inter-Varsity, 1973), p. 43.

2. Richard F. Lovelace, *Renewal as a Way of Life* (Downers Grove: Inter-Varsity, 1985), p. 178.

God's appointed vehicle for transforming people's lives. Repeatedly we have listened to students in our college classes report how important a word or deed from a caring Sunday school teacher was to them in their personal or spiritual development. Teachers can speak to the life situation of a student with words of grace in a way that books and mass media ministries rarely do.

The Teacher as Spiritual Liability

If the teacher's life and words can be a means of grace, they also have the opposite potential. While teachers can be signposts pointing students toward conversion and Christian growth, they can also be roadblocks that push people into spiritual detours and dead ends. God is not the only spiritual force in the universe who uses people. The sound words of the Christian teacher foster growth. Other words always remain a possibility.

Years ago, a cartoon showed two frames, each with a Mr. Brown talking with a young woman in his office. In the first frame he's a public school superintendent, and he says, "I'm awfully sorry, Miss Smith, but after reviewing your application for a teaching position, we've decided we can't use you. We must have someone with at least five years' experience in teaching and preferably with a master's degree in education."

In the second frame Mr. Brown is a Sunday school superintendent and he says, "You'd make a *wonderful* teacher, Miss Smith. I realize you haven't been a Christian very long, and you feel you don't know much about the Bible—but there's no finer way to learn the Bible than to teach it. And you say you have no experience working with kids in this age group—but I'm convinced you'll grow to understand and love them. Really, Miss Smith, all we're looking for is a willing heart."

Howard G. Hendricks, *Teaching to Change Lives* (Portland: Multnomah, 1987), p. 16.

We recall a small meeting in which faculty members were struggling valiantly with the question of what teachers want their students to be like. Vague, platitudinous answers carried the day until someone proposed an answer that shocked the group. That answer was, "We want our students to be like us." The answer ended the discussion. It was so straightforward as to offend and seemed to bespeak an unhealthy self-satisfaction.

After the initial shock had worn off, we realized the truthfulness of the idea. If teachers do not expect students to become like them—to share their understanding of the truth and their values—they are obviously frauds. If teachers believe in what they are teaching, of course they want to be emulated by their students. The desire to influence students is basic to teaching.

But something in this desire makes us uncomfortable. For one thing, teachers often disagree among themselves about what constitutes the truth. They attempt to influence students in conflicting directions. Obviously not all of these directions can be the right ones. Then, too, as teachers we are aware of the gap between what we profess as true and the ways in which our own behavior fails to measure up to that truth. We know within ourselves what maimed people we often are. How can the maimed produce healthy students?

While this is not a reason to abandon the teacher's calling, it is a fact to be acknowledged. Jesus reserved some of his harshest criticism for the religious teachers of his day. He prefaced his most scathing attack on them with the comment, "Practice and observe whatever they tell you, but not what they do; for they preach, but do not practice" (Matt. 23:3).

On another occasion Jesus warned that students tend not to rise above the spiritual level of their teachers:

> Can a blind man lead a blind man? Will they not both fall into a pit? A disciple is not above his teacher, but every one when he is fully taught will be like his teacher. [Luke 6:39–40]

Teachers could not avoid influencing their students if they tried. The influence is conscious and unconscious,

intended and unintended. The responsibility is momentous. This is no doubt what led James to write, "Let not
many of you become teachers...for you know that we
who teach shall be judged with greater strictness. For we
all make many mistakes" (James 3:1–2).

The Well-Rounded Teacher

Several years ago, an influential author reported that
modern society is marked by both "high tech" and "high
touch."[3] In such a world, teaching frequently looks dull
and outmoded, since it is neither high tech nor high
touch. It is not high tech because it is intensely human-
oriented. And it is something other than high touch because a teacher is always interested in truth as well as
human relationships.

Any sensitive teacher will feel the pull between relationships and instruction, between people and course
content. Students whose lives are busy and filled with
pressure yearn for caring relationships. In some churches,
one would almost be embarrassed to mention that the
major intent of a Sunday school class or Bible study is
studying the Bible, since this would be seen as a failure to
be sensitive to the life situations of people. Yet students
need to be taught as well as cared for. Teachers, moreover,
need to be convinced that often their teaching of the Word
of God is the most caring and compassionate thing they
can do.

The Inadequacy of
One-Dimensional Teachers

Research clearly shows that no single teacher attribute
or technique stands out as *the* mark of the effective
teacher. The marks of effective teaching generally tran-
scend specific teaching methods, teacher personalities,

3. John Naisbitt, *Megatrends: Ten New Directions Transforming Our Lives*
(New York: Warner, 1982), p. 39.

Figure 1 Two-Dimensional Model of Teaching*

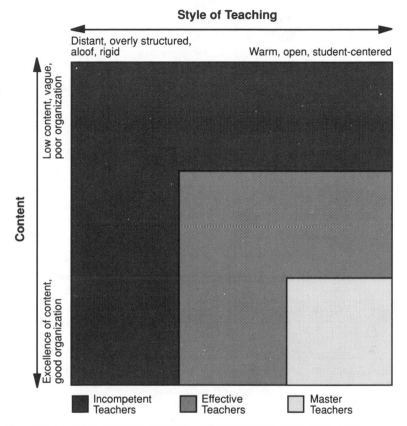

*Based on J. Lowman, *Mastering Techniques of Teaching* (Jossey-Bass, 1984), p. 20.

and instructional technologies. They cluster around two major dimensions of education: *interpersonal rapport* and *intellectual substance*. Effective teachers combine both dimensions. In Christian education settings, especially, teachers must exhibit strengths in both areas. The diagram in figure 1 shows how to evaluate a teacher in these areas.

Good teachers engender a warm, supportive class atmosphere *and* have the ability to communicate mastery of a subject in a stimulating way. This is where the specimen teachers we introduced in our opening chapter show their deficiencies. They both fall into the "incompetent" zone, which would come as quite a shock to Mary's students.

Students describe Bob as knowledgeable, clear, and organized. He knows the Bible thoroughly and enters the classroom prepared to share his detailed information with his class. But poor interpersonal skills diminish the usefulness of Bob's precise and encyclopedic knowledge. His teaching style lacks vitality and energy. It has little appeal and requires students to expend enormous sums of mental energy to stay attuned during class. In one-on-one encounters, people find him funny and engaging, but he is so caught up with efficiently transmitting large amounts of Bible facts to his class that he is "willing to give up some things." One of the things he gives up is dynamic interaction with the class.

Mary fails in the opposite way. She has an imprecise knowledge of the Bible and is convinced that, because she "learned a lot of verses as a kid that [she] never used," Bible knowledge has little to do with Christian maturity. She is an educational "romantic" who places great stock in "touching other lives" by sharing and discussion.

Mary has little to offer her students by way of content or perspective. Yet people flock to her class because they find it appealing, affirming, and supportive. Their glowing reports contradict what we might expect, since the overwhelming majority of the class say they go to the class first for Bible teaching and secondly for fellowship. But this cannot possibly be true, for there is little actual contact with the Bible during the class sessions. What the class actually shows is that in our fast-paced society people hanker for classes that show a concern for them and present material in a lively manner.

The Ideal of Multidimensional Teachers

Teachers can eliminate the tug-of-war between relationships and course content by being versatile and balanced. On the one hand, good teaching is characterized by interesting and significant content. *Knowledge* remains the starting point for effective teaching. H. L. Mencken no doubt overstated the case when he said that "a man who knows a subject thoroughly, a man so soaked in it that he eats it, sleeps it and dreams it—this man can always teach it with success, no matter how little he knows of technical pedagogy."[4] But the wisdom that underlies the statement remains valid: polished teaching techniques can never compensate for lack of content.

> It is the consensus of virtually all the men and women who have been working on curriculum projects that making material interesting is in no way incompatible with presenting it soundly; indeed, a correct general explanation is often the most interesting of all.
>
> Jerome S. Bruner, *The Process of Education* (Cambridge: Harvard University Press, 1977), p. 23.

But teachers need more than knowledge of their subject. They also need *enthusiasm*. People learn best from teachers who care about what they teach. Enthusiasm describes a teacher's infectious love for a subject. Teachers who care deeply about a subject not only teach the subject with an evident passion but also pass their love for the subject on to their students. Enthusiasm should not be confused with theatrics or grandstanding. The quiet enthusiasm of teachers who simply radiate their enchantment with the subject helps to make those teachers effective.

Engagement of students is another quality of good teachers. Good instruction draws students into active learning. Educational research has shown again and again that students learn best when they enter into class activities and take as active a role in learning as the teacher does in teaching.

4. H. L. Mencken, *Prejudices: Third Series* (New York: Knopf, 1922), p. 13.

> Classrooms are fundamentally dramatic arenas in which the teacher is the focal point, just as the actor or orator is on a stage. The students are subject to the same influences—both satisfactions and distractions—as any audience....Teaching is undeniably a performing art. Excellent teachers use their voices, gestures, and movements to elicit and maintain attention and to stimulate students' emotions. Like other performers, teachers must convey a strong sense of presence, of highly focused energy. Some teachers do this by being overtly enthusiastic, animated, or witty, while others accomplish the same effect with a quieter, more serious and intense style. The ability to stimulate strong positive emotions in students separates the competent from the outstanding...teacher.
>
> Joseph Lowman, *Mastering the Techniques of Teaching* (San Francisco: Jossey-Bass, 1984), p. 12.

Empathy is yet another trait that a teacher needs. Students are not just containers waiting to be filled with facts. They are people whose lives and personalities influence their learning. Teachers need to appreciate the context of their students' lives. They need to identify with the problems and preoccupations of the class members before whom they stand. They also need to be open to challenges and insights from their classes.

Good teachers also *challenge* their students to think and act beyond their current levels of achievement. To accomplish this goal, teachers need to be not only knowledgeable but also wise. Wisdom is more than the accumulation of Bible facts. It includes the ability to compare one's life and priorities with Scripture. Effective teachers challenge students to question and improve where they currently are in their spiritual walks. The teaching of such teachers is life-changing, not simply enthusiastic and clear in presentation.

The Passions of the Effective Teacher

We cannot stereotype the ideal Bible teacher. Good teachers use different methods, possess a wide range of personalities, express their care for class members in very different ways, incorporate media in differing degrees, and vary in the ways by which they establish rapport with a class. While good Bible teachers differ markedly in the way they teach, they share some common passions and orientations. How some people come to possess these traits, and how they can rekindle them when they have grown dull, remains shrouded in mystery. Yet these passions are at the heart of what it means to be gifted by the Holy Spirit to teach.

Good teachers have *a passion for people*. Teaching, after all, is a relational activity. "What subject do you teach?" is the standard question which follows when someone is introduced to a teacher. One of our colleagues likes to respond, "I don't teach a subject—I teach students." This is, of course, an overstatement, but a lot of teachers who are studious by temperament and who have an impressive grasp of a subject make poor teachers because they do not relate well to people.

Studying in preparation for a class presentation is a solitary activity. The result is that teaching often attracts introverted, studious people to its ranks. Good teachers have learned to balance their solitary delight in learning with the ability to be interested in people and their needs.

A passion for people must of course be supplemented by *a passion for the truth*. Good teachers believe in the momentous importance of the knowledge that they teach. The fastest way for teachers to bore their classes is to talk about something that they themselves do not regard as important or interesting. Every teacher occasionally experiences arid moments of this type, and they are to be counted among the nightmares of teaching. A good teacher stands before a class convinced that the content of the lesson is something terribly important.

It follows, therefore, that *a passion for study and learning* also characterizes the ideal teacher. Study forms the bedrock on which effective teaching is built. It lacks the glamor that many other ministries possess. Anyone who lacks the commitment to study should not teach. One of us knew a Bible-study leader who prepared so diligently that he often set aside his favorite pastime of watching sports in order to insure that he had studied thoroughly. Such a passion for study begets confidence in the teacher's calling. By contrast, a teacher's credibility is undermined by stories of throwing a Sunday lesson together between eleven and midnight on Saturday night.

But a passion for study does not by itself produce a good teacher. It must be accompanied by *a passion to share what the teacher has learned*. Many people are content to master a field for their own interest. The teacher's instinct consists of not being satisfied until one's knowledge has been enthusiastically shared. For the true teacher, this impulse is overwhelming. Not to be able to exercise the impulse is like having an arm or leg missing. The English writer Geoffrey Chaucer captured an important part of the essence of good teaching in his magical line about the Oxford student on a pilgrimage to Canterbury: "Gladly would he learn, and gladly teach."

The effective teacher also has *a passion for practical application of what is taught*. The goal of teaching is more than simply a grasp of truth detached from daily living. Master teachers want to see their students use what they have learned. They are interested in drawing connections between the Bible and the lives of their students, and they accordingly find ways to add the human touch to their teaching of the Bible. Students quickly sense that such teachers are in contact with life as they, too, know it.

A final passion of the ideal teacher is one that is the most important of all, yet one about which we do not talk much: the teacher must have *a passion for God*. The teacher's task in Bible teaching is to introduce people to a friend. It goes without saying that whenever we do not know someone well whom we are introducing to a third party, the introduction becomes inept and embarrassing. The goal of Bible teaching is more than the inculcation of a set of doctrines or moral principles. It is to facilitate the student's relationship to God.

The passions of the teacher are essential for effective Bible teaching. In general we do not hear enough about them in discussions of teaching. Yet they are one of the best yardsticks by which to measure a teacher's adequacy or inadequacy. When judged by that yardstick, many teachers need to reconsider their current practices as teachers, and perhaps whether they should be teaching at all. Conversely, this same list of qualifications should encourage people who do not currently teach to get into the act, since they obviously possess the right traits and abilities.

Our list of passions also raises the question of whether good teachers are made or born. This entire book is based on the premise that effective teaching can be nurtured through acquisition of the right skills, orientations, and tools of interpretation. But we cannot avoid the conclusion that there is something mysterious and "given" about how a person attains the status of a good teacher. To some degree, the right ingredients have to be present before a person can acquire the skills related to teaching.

Three Myths About the Effective Teacher

In this chapter we have sought to clarify what makes a teacher effective. An important part of such a process is clearing the air of some common misconceptions about successful teaching.

Myth #1: To be a good teacher, you have to be a brilliant classroom performer. Again and again we are surprised to observe what kind of lay teacher elicits positive responses from students. Rarely do we encounter a classroom spellbinder who can make a class hang on every word, each one of which seems to be loaded with remarkable insight. The norm is instead a rather ordinary person who consistently teaches biblical truth and applies it to life.

Good teaching is like good home cooking. We do not judge home cooking by the same standards we have for a gourmet banquet. Home cooking must be consistently tasteful, balanced, and nutritious. It does not have to be lavishly beautiful and stunningly striking. We probably do not even remember an ordinary meal two days later. Its quality is measured by the nutrition it supplies over the long haul, as well as by its availability and tastefulness.

Teachers would do well to remember the words of William Carey, the pioneer missionary to India. Carey's missionary career was astoundingly successful, yet he described himself as a "plodder." Most good Bible teachers are plodders. They edify their students, not through brilliant lessons (which they may, however, occasionally achieve), but by serving healthy words, week in and week out, through thoughtful study of the Bible.

Why choose either the ignorant enthusiast or the educated sluggard? Enthusiasm is not confined to the unskilled and the ignorant, nor are all calm, cool men idlers. There is an enthusiasm born of skill—a joy in doing what one can do well—that is far more effective, where art is involved, than the enthusiasm born in vivid feeling. The steady advance of veterans is more powerful than the mad rush of raw recruits. The world's best work, in the schools as in the shops, is done by the calm, steady, and persistent efforts of skilled workmen who know how to keep their tools sharp, and to make every effort reach its mark.

John Milton Gregory, *The Seven Laws of Teaching*, rev. ed. (Grand Rapids: Baker, 1954), pp. 22–23.

Living in a culture of personality cults and superheroes, we have mistakenly been led to judge effective teachers by an impossibly high standard of dazzling classroom performance. Most effective teachers are people who have taken the time to analyze their abilities, build upon their strengths, and find resources that will augment their weaknesses. We should discard our image of the teacher as charismatic performer who overwhelms a class with sheer forcefulness of personality. We should replace it with the image of the teacher as facilitator of class learning.

Myth #2: It is possible to identify the one best method of teaching. This myth is extremely prevalent. It underlies many published curriculum materials, and it influences whether a candidate is hired for a Christian education position. One of us recalls serving as a consultant and being told repeatedly by the person in charge that "everyone knows that the discussion format produces more effective learning."

The assumption that the discussion method or the lecture method or any other method produces the best

results cannot be confirmed by modern educational research. There is no one best way of teaching. Effective
teaching comes in many different formats.

By way of analogy, we might note how this applies in
the realm of architecture. Louis Sullivan, Chicago archi-
tect and mentor of Frank Lloyd Wright, popularized the
phrase that "form follows function." He meant by this
that the purpose of a building should influence its design
and style. Buildings should not be built in accordance
with some "perfect plan" that fits all buildings. Railroad
stations, banks, and schools should look different from
each other because they serve different purposes.

Good teaching adapts itself to many variables. The size
of the class, the nature of the room, the degree of interest
that students bring to the class, the age and life experiences of students, and the applicability of the subject
matter all influence the teaching format that good teachers use. Good teachers realize that trends and situations
and students keep changing as the years unfold. What
worked well a decade ago may be obsolete today. Even
within the life span of an individual teacher, there is no
"one right way" of teaching.

Myth #3: Good teachers are extroverts. All of us have
been subjected to enough boring class sessions that we
can easily reach the wrong conclusion that good teachers
are extroverts who find it easy to share themselves and
entertain people. It is true that extroverts have an advantage in fostering a caring environment in which learning
occurs. After all, such people gush with good will and find
it easy to demonstrate their feelings.

Teachers who are less demonstrative and who find it
uncomfortable to empathize publicly with the struggles
of students have to work harder at generating a warm,
caring class environment. But they are not disqualified
from the circle of effective teachers because they are
more reserved in their style of relating to others. They,

too, can find ways of showing concern, and often these are deeper than the potentially self-centered flamboyance of the extrovert. Simple things like remembering names and personal details, writing notes of encouragement, and being accessible before and after class show a teacher's concern for the lives of students.

There is an additional reason why people who are reserved in ordinary situations should not be disqualified (or disqualify themselves) from the opportunity to teach. The teacher in the classroom is not always the same person as the person out of the classroom. Given the position of teacher, some people come alive with a commanding presence that we could never have predicted from their out-of-class behavior.

Understanding the Life Cycles of Teaching

Many misconceptions about teaching, as well as some unnecessary self-laceration that teachers inflict, are eliminated when we understand that teachers undergo life cycles in their teaching. In fact, every class, as well as every class year, has an identifiable life cycle.

The Life Cycle of a Class

Classes and Bible studies live a life of their own. They are more like organisms than organizations. Like other organisms, they follow a predictable rhythm that needs to be understood by both teachers and students.

School teachers see this life cycle re-enacted every academic year. School years begin with hope and enthusiasm which fade as the year proceeds. New books become worn. New clothes lose their luster. Notebooks accumulate food spots.

Sunday school classes and Bible-study groups go through a similar (though less sharply marked) cycle. At the beginning, enthusiasm runs high. Teachers find it easy to prepare diligently. Class attendance is high. People are excited and eager to learn. This initial enthusiasm never completely sustains itself. It becomes muted into a period of realism. Teachers and students unconsciously adjust their expectations accordingly.

The period of realism is the crucial test for every class, every teacher, every student. It can turn in one of two directions. One is a kind of weariness, accompanied by a disappointed recognition that the class has not jelled and is failing to keep its initial promise. The other possibility is that the beginning enthusiasm matures into a sense of accomplishment about what has been learned and applied. The loss of the early excitement is accepted with regret, but not with hopelessness. In fact, there is a quiet regret that the class must end.

This life cycle is inevitable in a class. Skilled teachers know how to read the progress of a particular class. They do not lacerate themselves when the initial enthusiasm fades. Instead they look for ways to channel that enthusiasm into more mature understandings of the subject being covered.

One of the most important principles to note is that unduly long courses or units are self-defeating. We live in a day of short attention spans. People expect their experiences to be organized into relatively small segments. In general, the topics of Bible studies and Sunday school units should be organized into units of eight to twelve weeks. Teachers would do well to devise ways to break their units into discrete segments, even though the members of the group usually remain constant throughout the year.

The Rhythm of Education

The life cycle of an individual class is part of a much bigger phenomenon known as the rhythm of education. We borrow the phrase from the title of an essay by Alfred

North Whitehead.[5] Whitehead divides the process of education into the three stages of romance, precision, and generalization. This process is not so much the overall progress of people during their years of schooling as it is a description of the stages through which we go when mastering any subject. Whitehead stresses that "education should consist in a continual repetition of such cycles. Each lesson in its minor way should form an eddy cycle issuing in its own subordinate process."

The teacher's first task is to engender *romance and exploration.* This is the stage of grand introduction—the first vision of how vital and challenging the subject under consideration is. Here the subject under examination produces its own vitality and wonder born of novelty. The teacher's job at this stage is to open the student's mind to the wonder of the subject and invite the learners to see how important, how vast, and how marvelously intricate the subject is.

The next task of the teacher is the need for *precision.* This includes coming to grips with the facts of the subject being studied. Whitehead describes it as "the stage of precise progress when we acquire...facts in a systematic order, which thereby form both a disclosure and an analysis of the general subject matter romance." Initial excitement, glorious but without adequate understanding of the subject, now merges into sheer mastery of the field.

The final phase of learning a subject is the *stage of generalization.* Having mastered the data, students can now "put it all together" and supply overriding frameworks for the individual details. Here the big patterns underlying the study come into view. Having passed through the wonder of romance and mastered a subject through precision, students are able to see the big ideas and (even more importantly) make connections between those ideas and their own lives. In this stage people see the importance and relevance of what they have learned.

5. Alfred North Whitehead, "The Rhythm of Education," in *The Aims of Education* (New York: Macmillan, 1929, 1967), pp. 15–28.

PART 2

The Methods
of Effective
Bible Teaching

4

Teaching the Big Idea

In a previous chapter we noted that the commonest complaint about sermons in a survey of churchgoers was "too many ideas." It is also one of the most prevalent failures in Bible teaching. The reason many Bible lessons lack impact is that they do not have a single focus around which the lesson is built.

Happily this is one of the easiest problems to correct. The problem itself arises because teachers have never been told how important it is to formulate a summary statement of what a Bible passage says. We believe that teachers can improve their teaching almost overnight once they realize the need to organize their understanding of a biblical passage around a central insight. In this chapter we plan to outline and illustrate how to formulate the "big idea" in a biblical passage.

The Big Idea: Topic and Theme

There is no single "correct" way to formulate the big idea in a biblical passage. A survey of handbooks shows that people do not use the same terms when defining the issue. There are, however, some universal principles involved, as the following discussion will show.

Handbooks on preaching contain helpful suggestions. The need to formulate a statement of the big idea is one of the greatest strengths of Haddon W. Robinson's book *Biblical Preaching*.[1] Robinson's preferred terms are *subject* and *complement*. The subject is what a biblical passage is about. The complement completes the idea by stating what the passage says *about* that subject. Robinson is particularly concerned with the need to have a discernible subject and complement in sermons, but the same principles apply to teaching a passage from the Bible.

Students of public speaking and preaching have argued for centuries that effective communication demands a single theme. Rhetoricians hold to this so strongly that virtually every textbook devotes space to a treatment of the principle. Terminology may vary—central idea, proposition, theme, thesis statement, main thought—but the concept is the same. . . . Since each paragraph, section, or subsection of Scripture contains an idea, an exegete does not understand a passage until he can state its subject and complement exactly. While other questions emerge in the struggle to understand the meaning of a biblical writer, the two—What is the author talking about? and What is he saying about what he is talking about?—are fundamental.

Haddon W. Robinson, *Biblical Preaching* (Grand Rapids: Baker, 1980), pp. 33–34, 41.

Robinson claims that preachers need to answer two questions: What am I talking about? What exactly am I saying about what I'm talking about? When we organize our understanding of a Bible passage, we can simply adapt those questions to the biblical author: What is he talking about? Exactly what does he say about that subject?

The methodology for stating the unifying focus of a Bible passage will also be clarified if we compare the process to writing an essay. From high school onward, we were told in writing courses that we must first decide on a

---

1. Haddon W. Robinson, *Biblical Preaching* (Grand Rapids: Baker, 1980), pp. 31–48.

topic and then narrow that topic down to a specific thesis. One writing handbook has a section entitled "From Subject to Thesis."[2] According to this source, the thesis is what a writer intends to assert *about* the subject. It should be stated as a complete sentence or proposition.

Another writing handbook speaks of beginning with a broad subject and then *narrowing it down* to a specific idea about the subject.[3] If, for example, a writer's broad subject is "housework," the thesis that would provide the specific focus for the essay might be that "housework is frustrating and boring." A common set of terms for the broad subject and its specific focus are *topic* and *theme.*

Yet another writing handbook describes the need for a controlling idea thus:

> Most essays are focused on and controlled by a single main idea that the writer wants to communicate to readers—a central theme to which all the general statements and specific information of the essay relate. This main idea, called the thesis, encompasses the writer's attitude toward the topic and purpose in writing.[4]

As this statement suggests, the thesis is what unifies an essay. Everything in an essay relates in some way to the central idea.

Of course the thesis of an essay is supported by a series of further generalizations. These, in fact, constitute the topic sentences of individual paragraphs. A good essay does not simply keep repeating the same idea. It breaks the thesis into its parts. But by formulating an umbrella statement that unifies the individual statements, writers insure that their essay will be unified by a single focus.

2. Sheridan Baker, *The Practical Stylist*, 6th ed. (New York: Harper and Row, 1985), pp. 19–24.

3. Barbara F. Clouse, *The Student Writer: Editor and Critic* (New York: McGraw-Hill, 1986), p. 33.

4. H. Ramsey Fowler, *The Little, Brown Handbook*, 3d ed. (Boston: Little, Brown, 1986), p. 24.

Why bring up essay writing in a discussion of teaching the Bible? Because effective teaching of a Bible passage has something important in common with a good essay: it makes a central assertion *about* the material under consideration. It is not enough to simply choose a single passage for a Bible study. We also need a *thesis* for the passage and the lesson.

A good Bible study shares important features with a good essay. All that the following writer says about a well-constructed essay applies equally to a well-structured Bible study.

The *topic*...determines the area you are going to cover; the *thesis* determines the route you are going to take through that area. Without a thesis a paper inhabits a certain territory, but is likely to drift aimlessly like a purposeless vagrant. However interesting or well-written such a paper may be, a reader cannot help but wonder: What's the point? How does all of this connect? What am I supposed to come away with? A sharply focused thesis gives a paper direction, gives it a goal to aim for.

Bruce Bawer, *The Contemporary Stylist* (New York: Harcourt Brace Jovanovich, 1987), p. 13.

We will do a better job of preparing a Bible study if we grasp the parallel between our preparation and the writing of an essay. A good Bible study, too, has a unifying focus based on the content of a biblical passage. If a teacher has not wrestled with the concepts in a chapter of the Bible and come up with a unified statement, the class will not understand that the passage has unity.

Practical Suggestions

When preparing a Bible study, arrive as early as possible at an understanding of the big idea that governs the passage. Then slant the entire lesson around that central focus.

It works best to use a two-step process in stating the big idea of a passage. The first step consists of identifying the broad topic or concept that names what the passage is about. The second step is to narrow that topic down to a specific idea that the passage asserts about the broad subject. The most widely accepted terms for these two elements are *topic* (or *subject*) and *theme* (or *thesis*).

In most cases, the final statement should be a complete sentence or proposition, though there are exceptions to this rule, as we shall see.

Illustrations of Formulating the Big Idea

To illustrate what we have been saying, we have selected three specimens of the three main types of writing in the Bible, as follows:

Didactic exposition: 1 Corinthians 13, James 1, and Deuteronomy 10:12–22

Lyric poetry: Psalms 46, 64, and 139

Story or narrative: Genesis 3, Judges 4, and Acts 16:11–40

We have briefly reconstructed the process by which we arrived at our statements, and we have indicated the acceptable range of possibilities that exists when different people look at the same passage.

Didactic Exposition

1 Corinthians 13 The unifying topic is obviously love. But what does the chapter say *about* love? The passage falls into three distinct units: the indispensability of love (vv. 1–3), the acts and attributes of love (vv. 4–7), and the permanence of love that makes it superior to other Christian qualities (vv. 8–13). Faced with this multiplicity, one of us chose this as the unifying idea of the passage: *Because of its excellence, love should be the mark of a Christian.* The other stated the matter thus: *Love is indispensable to the Christian life.*

These statements are very similar. They both push a Bible study toward treating the passage as descriptive of a model of behavior that every Christian is expected to exhibit. They are also broad enough to cover the range of individual topics covered within the chapter.

But we should also note a problem that the teacher would have to solve: the concept that love is *excellent* or *indispensable* is so general that the teacher would have to be aggressive in doing justice to the specificity of the individual units within the chapter. This is a rather common situation, and the teacher should often expect a creative tension between the need to keep a Bible study tied to an overriding framework and the need to get close to the specifics of a text.

James 1 We chose this chapter because it typifies the miscellaneous mixture and range of topics found in many a chapter in the Bible, especially in the New Testament. There is simply no way to get around the fact that the writer of this passage changes the topic every two or three verses. Usually the unifying topic of such a chapter in the Epistles can be stated as *practical Christian living*, or something similar.

One of us was impressed by the high proportion of James 1 that is phrased in the form of commands, and therefore stated the big idea of the chapter as: *God has given us commands to guide us in practical Christian living*. The other's formulation was: *True religion is demonstrated by our response to circumstances*. This is a much more specific slant on the chapter. It grew out of an awareness that the chapter has a lot to say about trials and about the tangible witness of true religion. An appropriate teaching strategy is to focus on how important proper responses are in the Christian life.

This suggests that our formulation of topic and theme might well be a choice from among available options. It will often be guided by what we wish to accomplish in a given meeting, or by the nature and needs of the group. A pitfall that teachers need to avoid is seizing upon something that is important in just one part of a passage but does not fit other parts. The last third of James 1, for example, has much to say about our speech, but it would be a liability to try to slant a discussion of the whole chapter around that topic.

Deuteronomy 10:12–22 Many of the direct teaching passages in the Bible are embedded in narrative books in the form of speeches. This is how the teaching of Jesus appears in the Gospels. The passage we selected from Deuteronomy is part of Moses' farewell address to the Israelites. It is a somewhat miscellaneous series of commands, beginning with the famous verse, "And now, Israel, what does the LORD your God require of you, but to fear the LORD your God. . . ."

Because the passage consists largely of commands, both of us seized upon the idea of God's requirements as the topic. Our statements of theme were also similar: *Because God has been faithful to his people, he requires that they demonstrate their faithfulness in return;* and, *God requires that we love and obey him.*

When a passage is as miscellaneous in its structure as this one, it is helpful to break it into constituent parts under the format of *theme and variation*. The individual parts are variations on the main theme. We could go through the passage unit by unit and identify specific variations on the theme of what God requires of us or why he requires it.

Lyric Poetry

Psalm 46 With Psalm 46 we move into the genre of lyric poetry. Poems are structured similarly to expository prose and can be organized according to the theme-and-variation scheme. Psalm 46 is structured as a continuous contrast between the threatening events going on around us (all the way from erosion and earthquakes to international warfare) and the calm certainty of God's control of the world. Any statement of the unifying focus will in some sense deal with this contrast.

One of us chose *God's presence amid troubling times* as the topic. Narrowed down more specifically, the psalm asserts *the security and confidence that come from trusting God's presence amid troubling times.* The other's statement similarly focused on the central contrast in the poem and the effect that this has on the person who believes in God: *God's presence in calamity gives us strength and delivers us from fear.*

We might notice that a person's formulation of topic and theme should arise from an adequate grasp of the genre (literary type) and structure of a passage. The big idea depends on accurate analysis of a text. In the case of Psalm 46, the statements that we came up with were based on our analysis of the central contrast in the poem, and, in keeping with the fact that it is a lyric poem that expresses feelings, they stress the emotional response or feeling underlying the poem.

Psalm 64 This is a short psalm, but the fact that it is a lament psalm makes it complex. A lament psalm almost always has five parts (which can appear in any order): cry to God, lament or complaint (a description of the crisis), petition to God for help, statement of confidence in God, and a vow to praise God. What principle is large enough to cover all these elements? In particular, how can we find unity in a poem that contains a recantation in which the speaker reverses his opening premise that his situation is virtually hopeless?

An answer begins to emerge when we realize that a lament psalm can always be viewed as containing the speaker's response to a crisis, combined with a strategy for mastering that crisis. On the basis of this principle, one of us formulated the topic of Psalm 64 as *the hostility of evil people*, and the theme as *we can trust God to help us when we are victimized by malicious people.* This formulation covers both the cry of helplessness and the statement of confidence in God. To propose a statement that covers only one of these would be insufficient.

The other's formulation was likewise rooted in the fact that this is a lament psalm. The topic is *responding to personal attacks*, and the specific theme is that *God will vindicate those who trust him and punish their attackers according to his own timing.*

We might note in passing that it would be natural to phrase the topic in terms of the threat that *the speaker* faced. While this is no doubt the terminology that we would use when actually interacting with the psalm, the statement of the main idea should be stated in *universal terms* so that it includes not only the speaker but also the application that we would make to our own lives.

Psalm 139 This is a psalm of praise. The main ingredient in such a poem is the list or catalogue of God's praiseworthy acts. The catalogue usually covers a wide (and sometimes miscellaneous) range of God's acts, with the result that the unity of the psalm may be hard to state. We selected Psalm 139 for the additional reason that it illustrates the difficulties posed by a long psalm.

Psalm 139 is an exalted lyric poem that praises God's omniscience (vv. 1–6), omnipresence (vv. 7–12), creativity (vv. 13–18), and holiness (vv. 19–24). It is always possible to identify the topic in a psalm of praise as *God's praiseworthy character and acts*, and to state as the theme that *God is worthy of praise for his character and acts*. One of us was content with such a formulation. Although it is a very general idea, it is adequate to keep the four-part psalm tied to an overriding framework.

The other one of us viewed the psalm as dealing with *God's activity in the world*. The specific theme, in this view, is that *God is active everywhere in the world, so live accordingly*. This person considered but then rejected as too localized the topic "God knows everything." This would leave out sections of the poem dealing with God's creativity and holiness.

Narrative or Story

Genesis 3 Here we come to narrative or story. Genesis 3 is the story of a temptation and fall into sin. Often a story is best viewed as a *picture* or *anatomy* or *case study* of a certain type of experience, and it may be most natural to phrase the big idea of the story in those terms instead of trying to state it as a proposition having a subject and predicate.

One of us took the approach that Genesis 3 gives us a picture or anatomy of *how sin happens in a person's life*. In filling out a Bible study on this passage, one would then find ways to complete the formula *sin happens when....* (For example, when we disobey God, when we mistakenly think that sin has no price tag attached, when we allow ourselves to be deceived by Satan, and so forth.)

The other one of us took his cue from the fact that this is a story of temptation and a story of crime and its punishment. We might note again that our statement of topic and theme must be rooted in our analysis of the specific literary features of a passage. The resulting for-mulation of the topic is *a study in temptation*, while the theme is that *our response to temptation affects our futures*. The notion of temptation and consequences is true to how the story unfolds: it begins with the tempta-tion and then tells about the consequences. The focus on how our response to temptation affects our future is relatively specific. It thus illustrates the freedom that a teacher has to slant a study in a specific direction for purposes of a given meeting. We are obviously not in quest for *the* one right statement of topic and theme for every Bible passage.

Judges 4 This is the story of the defeat of the Canaanites by Deborah, Barak, and Jael. It is typical of the historical narratives in the Bible in being brief and self-contained. Yet it includes numerous characters, and the action falls into several distinct events. What is the unifying core of such a story? The best clue is to note the central *action*. In fact, the starting point for discerning the big idea in a story is simply to state in general terms what happens in the story.

Judges 4 tells the story of a national deliverance. We are given the background, context, occurrence, and aftermath of this rescue. If the story is thus about God's deliverance of a nation, what is the accompanying truth that the story teaches or embodies?

One of us saw the story as dealing with *God's providence*. That providence, moreover, works through ordinary human means, including political and military institutions and the resourcefulness of individuals like the tricky Jael. The final statement of theme was: *God accomplishes his work in the world through human institutions and the personal abilities of people.*

The other one of us preferred a more specific approach. He imagined a lesson designed for a leadership training class in the local church. The resulting statement of theme was *the importance of good leaders for God's people.* We can see again the need to formulate the topic and theme on the basis of teachability for a specific group and purpose.

We wish to emphasize that the topic and theme of a story must be stated *in universal terms* and should therefore be *distinguished from plot summary.* To say that "God delivered Israel through the courage of Deborah and Jael" is to summarize the plot but not to state a universal truth. To avoid plot summary, one should take care not to use the names of specific characters in the story.

Acts 16:11–40 This story of Paul's ministry, arrest, and rescue at Philippi is a typical specimen of biblical narrative. These stories always require an act of interpretation just to determine what they are about. An expository passage like 1 Corinthians 13 announces its topic, but a story is more indirect.

Most stories in the Bible are variations on the theme of God's providence in the world. One of us accordingly formulated the unity of this story as *God's providential care of his servants.* In actually teaching the passage, one would have to come up with further subordinate generalizations about *how* God cares for his servants.

The other one of us saw the story as dealing more specifically with *the witness of the gospel in the world.*

The theme, in this view, is that *although the preaching of the gospel meets resistance in the world, God is able to arrange events in such a way as to overcome these obstacles.*

We came to several conclusions while working with these passages, and they can serve as a summary of the principles underlying this chapter.

1. When stating the big idea that unifies a biblical passage, we are not necessarily in quest of *the* one right statement. The passages we discussed could be legitimately taken in several different directions. Some formulations may be more accurate or more helpful than others, but good interpreters will often produce differing statements for a given passage.

2. What, then, are the main criteria for assessing different statements of topic and theme? They are chiefly five. A good statement of topic and theme must provide a single focus for a passage, be brief enough to be manageable, be based on accurate analysis of the passage, cover the entire passage, and steer a middle course between undue generality (thereby ignoring the specificity of a passage) and excessive specificity (thereby limiting universality of application).

3. A statement of topic and theme should be linked to the audience and specific purpose for which a lesson is intended. A teacher might well choose to formulate the big idea on the basis of the capabilities of a class or the goal for a specific meeting. The statement might be influenced by the situation of a given group at a given time.

4. Our statement of the big idea of a passage requires that we give attention to the literary form of the passage. In explaining how we arrived at our statements, we repeatedly commented on the literary form of the passages.

5. The purpose of stating the topic and theme of a passage is to insure that a Bible study will be focused and unified. We need not agonize over one good option compared with another one. Which one we choose may, in fact, be slightly arbitrary. This is all right. The important thing is that a Bible study have a discernible point.

5

Bridging the Gap

From the opening chapter of the Book of Judges comes the following account: "Adoni-Bezek fled, but they chased him and caught him, and cut off his thumbs and big toes. Then Adoni-Bezek said, 'Seventy kings with their thumbs and big toes cut off have picked up scraps under my table. Now God has paid me back for what I did to them'" (vv. 6–7 NIV).

This gruesome episode highlights a problem facing any teacher of the Bible, namely, the remoteness of the biblical world from our own. The spectacle of people without thumbs and big toes scrambling around the table for scraps of food is not part of our daily reality. Even the names frequently accentuate the strangeness that we feel as we read the Bible. The Bible is obviously an ancient document, and customs change with the centuries.

A chief problem that every effective teacher of the Bible must solve is making the Bible accessible to the modern reader and showing how that world relates to our own experiences. The customary term for this is "bridging the gap." The gap is not equally large with every biblical passage. A passage like the following from a New Testament epistle states its content so directly that it means the same thing to us that it did to the original audience: "But now you must rid yourselves of . . . anger, rage, malice, slander, and filthy language from your lips. Do not lie to each other" (Col. 3:8–9 NIV). Here we are at the opposite end of the spectrum from the seventy kings without thumbs and big toes scrambling for scraps of food. Most passages in the Bible fall somewhere between these extremes.

Bridging the gap between our own world and the world of the Bible requires that we make a two-way journey. We begin by traveling from our own time and place to the ancient world of the Bible. Then we take a return trip to our own experience of life. Two questions govern our interpretation of a biblical text: What did it mean then? What does it mean now?

It is because preaching is not exposition only but communication...that I am going to develop...the metaphor...of bridge-building. Now a bridge is a means of communication between two places which would otherwise be cut off from one another by a river or a ravine....The chasm is the deep rift between the biblical world and the modern world....It is across this broad and deep divide of two thousand years of changing culture (more still in the case of the Old Testament) that Christian communicators have to throw bridges. Our task is to enable God's revealed truth to flow out of the Scriptures into the lives of the men and women of today.

John R. W. Stott, *Between Two Worlds: The Art of Preaching in the Twentieth Century* (Grand Rapids: Eerdmans, 1982), pp. 137–38.

A landmark essay on the subject is Krister Stendahl's article on contemporary theology in *The Interpreter's Dictionary of the Bible*.[1] Proposing that interpretation of the Bible must be governed by the two questions of "what it meant" and "what it means," Stendahl notes that in modern theology these two questions have tended to be in competition. That is, those biblical scholars who have been most thorough in the descriptive task of uncovering

---

1. Krister Stendahl, "Biblical Theology, Contemporary," in *The Interpreter's Dictionary of the Bible*, ed. George A. Buttrick, 4 vols. (Nashville: Abingdon, 1962), 1:418–32.

what the Bible meant in its original context have tended to seal the Bible off from contemporary relevance. On the other hand, those who are zealous to show the relevance of the Bible to modern life have been indifferent to the descriptive task of living inside a biblical text.

Contemporary preaching and Bible teaching show the same dichotomy, as do some published Bible curriculum materials. Many teachers dutifully share what they have learned about the background of a passage without adequately tackling the question of how the passage relates to daily living. Other teachers make the opposite mistake: they never make the journey from their own world to the world of the Bible. They are so intent on showing the spiritual or theological meaning of a text that they never enter the world of the text. We can note in passing that the common practice of moralizing or allegorizing the details in a passage is one of the commonest forms of this failure. A teacher who allegorizes the giant Goliath as Sin has not entered into the world of the story.

The Journey to the World of the Bible

The first task of the reader or teacher of the Bible is to *relive the text*. This means allowing ourselves to be transported from our own time and place to another time and place. During this journey we become self-forgetful as we temporarily leave our own world behind. The goal is to become a spectator or participant in a world far removed

---

The ideal interpreter should be one who has entered into that strange first-century world, has felt its whole strangeness, has sojourned in it until he has lived himself into it, thinking and feeling as one of those to whom the Gospel first came, and who will then return into our world, and give to the truth he has discovered a body out of the stuff of our own thought.

C. H. Dodd, *The Present Task in New Testament Studies* (Cambridge: Cambridge University Press, 1936), pp. 40–41.

from the world of asphalt parking lots and microwave ovens.

To do this requires the use of imagination. The imagination enables us to identify with things beyond ourselves. When we imagine, we vicariously enter a world and identify with characters and objects beyond our familiar world. We join ourselves with something "out there."

The imagination is also our image-making and image-perceiving capacity. It is our ability to picture reality concretely. As such it complements our abstract intellect, which is adept at dealing with propositions and general statements. When we enter the world of a biblical text, we need to picture as much as possible.

The World of the Biblical Text

The world of the biblical text that we enter by an act of imagination is made up of several things. One is simply the literal, physical properties of that world. In a story these are settings, characters, and actions. In poetry they are the abundance of physical images and sensations that are the essential language of the poet. Visionary or prophetic writing tends to combine the elements of story and poetry, with the result that we are brought into an encounter with people and events as well as concrete images.

To relive a biblical text therefore requires first of all the ability to picture the tangible elements named in the text. In terms popularized by contemporary psychology, we need to read with the right side of the brain—the hemisphere that is active when we think in pictures. At this initial stage of dealing with a biblical text, we should not be preoccupied with finding the spiritual meaning of the passage. We should feel quite free to pay attention to things that on the surface seem remote from any spiritual importance.

In addition to literal foreground details and sensations, the world of a biblical text consists of the cultural context

out of which the text comes and which is presupposed by the writer. This cultural context includes customs or practices prevalent in the writer's world. Psalm 23, for example, repeatedly draws upon the activities that a shepherd would perform for his sheep during the course of a typical day. The shepherd would lead his sheep on safe paths through rough terrain to midday rest in a shady place. He would protect them from predators (the "enemies" in whose presence the sheep eat [v. 5]) and would anoint scratches with olive oil at the sheepfold at the end of the day. Reconstructing such practices prevalent in the world portrayed in a biblical text is not optional; it is the necessary first step in understanding and teaching a passage from the Bible.

The world of a biblical text also includes the ideas or attitudes accepted by the author and the characters in the text. Jesus' parable of the good Samaritan is an example. The impact of the parable depends on our realizing that neighborly compassion comes from the least likely source. The Samaritans were the object of severe racial prejudice on the part of the Jews. That a Samaritan would show compassion to the wounded man, especially after the religious elite of Jewish society had passed by on the other side, was as unthinkable (given current prejudices) as a compassionate Muslim might be to us.

Or consider the story in which Abraham intercedes on behalf of Sodom and Gomorrah (Gen. 18:16–33). Abraham appeals to God's sense of justice. This implies an attitude toward deity that is taken for granted during the course of the conversation. But when we turn to other stories from the ancient world, we find such an assumption absent. The ways of the gods in these stories are arbitrary and mysterious. Entering into the world of any story requires that we note the attitudes presupposed by the writer and characters in the story.

Travel Guides to the World of the Text

The most effective aids in traveling to the world of the biblical text are without doubt visual images of that world. These need not be limited to the conventional Holy Land pictures. There is much that is universal in the world of biblical texts. We can make the nature psalms come alive with slides from our family vacations.

Visual images come in various forms. One is simply physical objects that a teacher takes to class. Slides are also especially effective. If a group is small, pictures in books can be held up or circulated. If these resources are impossible, one can use words to create imagined scenes.

Geography plays a major role in many parts of the Bible. Maps are always a relevant source with such passages. Relating geographical facts from the ancient world to familiar distances, population figures, and so forth is likewise effective. If the Red Sea is twelve hundred miles long and two hundred miles wide, students find it useful to know what this means when plotted in terms of familiar geography.

Commentaries and Bible dictionaries are gold mines of information about the world of a biblical text. These are essential among a Bible teacher's tools. The most helpful commentaries are of course scholarly ones, as distinct from devotional or homiletic ones. Beyond that, there is no way other than browsing widely to know which commentaries will be good for reconstructing the world of a text. Even within the same commentary series one will find a wide range of adequacy on this matter.

There is today a general religious bias toward a galloping subjectivity. But our first obligation to a text is to let it hang there in celestial objectivity—not to ask what it means *to us*. A good sermon or a good teaching job must begin with angelic objectivity.

There's something in the mood of our culture that hates that. We want to hurry up and get to what something means to the individual. But this notion presents a serious danger for the true meaning of any important text—biblical, literary or otherwise. The text had a particular meaning before I saw it, and it will continue to mean that after I have seen it.

Joseph Sittler, "Provocations on the Church and the Arts," *Christian Century*, March 19–26, 1986, p. 294.

We should not overlook our own imaginations as resources to be used when getting inside the biblical world. The Bible contains far more appeals to the imagination (image-perceiving capacity) than we are usually aware. All we need to do is be active in picturing the details and following the cues laid down by the biblical text.

From the Bible to Our Own World

Effective bridging of the gap between our own world and the world of the Bible is a two-way trip. Having entered the world of the Bible, we need to make a return journey to our familiar world. In doing so, we are actually putting into practice a conventional rule of good teaching—using the familiar to explain the unfamiliar. The world of the Bible will cease to seem strange and remote if we can relate it to things in our own world.

The most helpful metaphor by which to view this process is the Bible teacher as translator. In relating the details of a biblical passage to familiar experience, the teacher does something analogous to what scholars do when they translate from one language to another. The translation occurs at several levels.

The Bible Teacher as Translator

One type of translation occurs when we state the details of the biblical text in our own language. We are not yet talking about finding modern counterparts for characters and events in the Bible, but rather about how we name those details. It is amazing how much falls into place if we simply find a familiar category in which to include it.

When Esther entered a pagan harem and was given a Persian name in addition to her Hebrew name, she underwent what today we call an identity crisis. After his greatest feat as a prophet (triumphing over the prophets of Baal), Elijah suffered a severe case of burnout. Joseph faced a predicament when his boss's wife wanted to have an affair with him. Once we start to name things in our idiom, they come alive for us. Without such translation, the world of the Bible remains remote from us.

A second type of translation is to find modern counterparts for details in the Bible. To catch the shock in Jesus' parable of the employer who paid the same wage to everyone regardless of how long they had worked, we can picture a teacher who gives all the students an A, no matter how much or how little they had studied. In Judges 7:13 we read about a Midianite's dream in which "a cake of barley bread tumbled into the camp...and came to the tent, and struck it so that it fell, and...lay flat." Cakes of barley bread are not exactly daily sights for us, but we can catch the force of the original dream, including the latent humor of the situation, if we imagine someone recounting a dream in which a loaf of bread landed on his camper and smashed it flat.

A third type of translation is to identify the recognizable human experience in a biblical text. Despite the remoteness of many of the practices and customs that we read about in the Bible, the Bible is filled with human experience as it has existed at all times and in all places. A newspaper is out of date two days later, but the Bible is always up to date. We can find common human experience at a number of levels in the Bible.

One is the physical level. As we read the Bible, for example, we are never far from the world of hunger and thirst and physical weariness. We read about people who suffer pain and who handle such tangible objects as swords and sheaves of grain. The poetry of the Bible, moreover, constantly appeals to the familiar physical sensations that make up our daily reality: "The ordinances of the Lord are...sweeter also than honey and drippings of the honeycomb" (Ps. 19:9–10).

We also encounter recognizable emotional experiences in the Bible, especially in its lyric poetry. Only a poet would express the matter in the following way, but anyone in love can understand the emotional experience portrayed:

> You have ravished my heart, my sister, my bride,
>   you have ravished my heart with a glance of your eyes,
>   with one jewel of your necklace. [Song of Sol. 4:9]

Similarly, we know all about the depression that the psalmist expresses in poetic form: "My bones burn like a furnace....I am like a lonely bird on the housetop" (Ps. 102:3, 7).

Stated or implied emotions are equally important in the stories of the Bible, though the spare, unembellished style in which these stories are written requires that we imagine the feelings of the characters in the stories. On the day on which Abraham set out on his trip to sacrifice Isaac, he rose early in the morning (Gen. 22:3). Why did he get up so early? For the same reason we get up early when we face a crisis—he had spent a sleepless night in his agony of heart. It is not hard to imagine the fear that Esther experienced as she stepped into the hall leading to the throne room of the king without having been summoned.

The emotions portrayed and implied in the Bible are one of the most consistent points of contact between it and us. There is an affective level of reality that can be used to bridge the gap between the biblical world and our own experience.

We can also find an abundance of recognizable human experience in the Bible at the moral level. Social settings and customs change with time, but moral realities remain the same. The circumstances surrounding the sudden deaths of Ananias and Sapphira were unique, but the moral experience of lying and thinking we can get by with it is universally human.

Joseph found himself employed by a man with such an odd name—Potiphar—that we could imagine him to be a fictional character in a fantasy story. But the strangeness of that world evaporates when we read, "Now Joseph was handsome and good-looking. And after a time his master's wife cast her eyes upon Joseph, and said, 'Lie with me'" (Gen. 39:6–7). The moral experience here is obviously sexual temptation.

We can also recognize a level of spiritual reality in the Bible, even in passages where the surface details are remote from our own experience. In the psalms of worship, for example, we encounter much that is foreign to our own worship experiences—pilgrimages to the temple, sacrifices, shouting, loud music, processions, and prayers for the king. But the spiritual experiences of encountering God in worship, being filled with awe before him, and delighting in corporate worship are thoroughly recognizable.

Another common type of experience that we find in abundance in the Bible is psychological experience. Consider, for example, the following account that David gives of his battle with unrelieved guilt:

> When I declared not my sin, my body wasted away
>   through my groaning all day long.
> For day and night thy hand was heavy upon me;
>   my strength was dried up as by the heat of summer.
>   [Ps. 32:3–4]

This is not, as one of us once thought, simply a bit of hyperbole. It is a nearly clinical analysis of David's state of mind and includes references to insomnia, psychosomatic ailments, stress, loss of appetite, and emotional fatigue.

We can also sense common human experience at the level of human relationships when we enter the world of the Bible. We encounter it, for example, in Jesus' parable of the prodigal son. When the older brother refuses the festivities at the end of the parable, complaining to his father about his brother's bad behavior, we know exactly what is happening. It is called sibling rivalry.

It is an easy step from the familiar human experience that we find in the Bible to the related phenomenon of archetypes. An archetype is an image, character type, or event that recurs throughout literature and life. Archetypes capture the universal, enduring elements of human experience. As we read the Bible, for example, we keep encountering images of light and darkness, journey and home, temptation and wilderness. These images are as much a part of our own lives as they are of the Bible and are a leading means by which we can show people the closeness of the Bible to their own experience.

A related category of bridge-building is to identify literary parallels between a biblical text and literature with which we are familiar. By means of such identification, biblical texts become recognizable and accessible. The story of Samson, for example, is like other tragedies we have read. King Saul's attempt to convince Samuel that he killed all the flocks of the Amalekites while the sheep and cattle provide a background chorus (1 Sam. 15:13–14) is the kind of material from which situation comedies on television are made.

A final avenue to bridging the gap between the biblical world and our own experience is application. Whenever we start to talk about how the experiences and ideas in a biblical passage apply to us, we are bridging the gap between "then" and "now." Having relived the experience of Peter's denial of Jesus, we need to ask what forms such temptations and denials take in our daily routine. Jonah's ironic attempt to run away from God may seem remote from anything that we literally do, but once we start to apply the principle of the event it is obvious that we, too, operate on the premise that God does not know what we are doing virtually every time we commit a known sin.

To sum up, the effective Bible teacher finds ways to relate the Bible to everyday life, making it in the process both accessible and relevant. The connections between those two worlds extend far beyond ideas. A wealth of human experiences and literary parallels also bind the Bible and our own lives together.

Integrating the Two Worlds

We have spoken of the double journey that the Bible teacher needs to make in bridging the gap between the Bible and the contemporary world. For people with the right skills, an alternative exists. It consists of integrating the two worlds in such a way that we live in both worlds simultaneously.

To illustrate what we mean, consider what a Bible teacher did with the parable of the two sons who were

asked to work in their father's vineyard. The parable is as
follows:

> A man had two sons; and he went to the first and said,
> "Son, go and work in the vineyard today." And he an-
> swered, "I will not"; but afterward he repented and went.
> And he went to the second and said the same; and he
> answered, "I go, sir," but did not go. Which of the two did
> the will of his father? [Matt. 21:28–31]

As we listen to the commentary of a Bible teacher on this
simple story, we simultaneously enter the world of the
story and bridge the gap to our own world:

> The problem of the first son is the problem of defiance.
> He too quickly opposes the will of his father. I would
> describe this boy in the following fashion: he is a big
> problem at breakfast, but a joy at supper....
> The second son is much more complicated. This boy is
> more slippery and evasive. Jesus pours it on with one little
> word, "I go, *sir*." He says what he thinks his father wishes
> to hear. He is a joy at breakfast, but a big problem at
> supper.
> You've all met this type. He says, "I'm awfully glad you
> suggested that I work in the vineyard, Father. You know, I
> was thinking this morning during quiet time, 'I would just
> love to work in the vineyard today.' After all, I realize
> we've got the vineyard so we can make money so all of us
> kids can go to college. I know that's part of the college
> fund. A family that works together stays together. Dad,
> thanks for the suggestion. Mother, put on another steak
> for me."[2]

On the one hand, the story itself comes alive in our
imaginations. We have been transported into the world of
the family portrayed in the story. But paradoxically we
have also been made aware of how that world relates to
our own. The family in the parable has become the family

---

2. Earl Palmer, chapel address at Wheaton College.

of our own experience and observation. The biblical
world and our own world have merged.

And as for the king of the kingdom himself [Jesus], whoever would
recognize him? He has no form or comeliness. His clothes are what he
picked up at a rummage sale. He hasn't shaved for weeks. He smells of
mortality. We have romanticized his raggedness so long that we can catch
echoes only of the way it must have scandalized his time in the horrified
question of the Baptist's disciples, "Are *you* he who is to come?" (Matt.
11:3); in Pilate's "Are you the king of the Jews?" (Matt. 27:11) you with
pants that don't fit and a split lip. . . .

Pilate lets the cigarette smoke drift out of his mouth to screen him a little
from the figure before him. Sarah tries to disguise her first choke of laughter
as a cough by covering her mouth with her apron, and Job sits at the table
with his head in his arms so that he won't have to face the empty chairs of
his children.

Frederick Buechner, *Telling the Truth: The Gospel as Tragedy, Comedy, and Fairy Tale*
(San Francisco: Harper and Row, 1977), pp. 90–91.

The ability to do this is limited to relatively few people
with unusually active imaginations. Even if this ability is
beyond us, such commentary highlights the goal of bridging the gap between the biblical and contemporary worlds
that every good Bible teacher achieves.

6

Discovering Unity
in Biblical Passages

To teach a passage effectively, a teacher must be able to communicate a sense of its unity. Educational research has shown that before people can grasp specific details they need a general framework to which they can relate the specific pieces of data. The implications for Bible teaching are immense, and unfortunately this is a somewhat neglected facet of books and courses.

Many published Bible-study materials, as well as most commentaries on the Bible, are weak in this area. They are far too atomistic in their approach. The unity of a Bible passage typically gets lost in a maze of verse-by-verse comments or questions. The same material, if carefully packaged in unifying frameworks, would have much more meaning for students.

The unity of a biblical passage consists of two distinct elements. One is thematic or conceptual unity, the idea that governs the passage. The other is structural unity, the unified progression by which a passage unfolds and forms a coherent whole.

Thematic Unity

The thematic unity of a passage is conceptual in nature. It is what in an earlier chapter we called the "big idea" of a passage. The theme is the main insight about life or the Christian faith that a passage asserts.

Many biblical passages of course embody or assert more than a single idea or theme. But for purposes of effective Bible teaching, it is important to choose one of these as the focus of attention. Building a lesson around a controlling theme is simply an effective teaching strategy.

Arriving at an understanding of the theme of a passage requires analysis and interpretation. Very few passages in the Bible come right out and state the unifying idea. This is something we have to formulate for ourselves as we come to understand a passage.

The methodology for arriving at a statement of theme is twofold. First we need to determine what the passage is about. The best clue is repetition: what does the writer continuously talk about in the passage? Answering that question is easier for expository (informational or explanatory) writing than for more literary texts such as poetry and story. This is because expository writing is itself conceptual. Poems and stories, by contrast, take human experience rather than ideas as their subject. To identify what a story or poem is about, therefore, we need to discover what human experience is portrayed.

The second step in formulating a statement of theme is to determine what the writer says *about* the unifying subject or human experience. This is the interpretive slant that the writer takes toward the subject. It is usually best stated as a complete sentence having a subject and predicate, as in this statement of theme for Psalm 23: God's people should live contentedly because God's providence in their lives is complete and sufficient.

Thematic Unity in Expository Passages

Thematic unity is the same for any type of passage, regardless of genre. In each case, the theme is a conceptual generalization or statement of truth. We cannot judge from the statement of theme itself whether the passage on which it is based is a piece of expository prose, a poem, or a story. But the means by which we arrive at an understanding of the theme is quite different for each of these three genres, as the following specimens suggest.

The Beatitudes of Jesus (Matt. 5:3–12) are expository. They consist of a series of assertions or propositions. Patterns of repetition tell us how to interpret the passage. The repeated formula *blessed are* alerts us that the passage is about the blessed person, or simply the ideal Christian.

What, then, does the passage assert about the blessed person? Answering this question requires analysis and interpretation. Again repetition is the best clue. What is the common denominator that unifies the individual beatitudes? If we look at the qualities of character that Jesus pronounces blessed, we find that they are spiritual qualities that run counter to what most people think make a person happy—such qualities as realizing one's spiritual poverty and being meek and pure in heart. This spiritual emphasis is reinforced when we look at the rewards that Jesus claims for the person being described—such rewards as inheriting the kingdom of heaven and seeing God. Putting this data together, we can formulate the theme of the Beatitudes something like this: God promises blessing to people who order their lives around spiritual values.

Arriving at such a statement of theme obviously requires some interpretive activity, but with expository writing this is relatively simple. The structure of an expository passage is a sequence of ideas. The ideas themselves are stated in a relatively straightforward way.

Thematic Unity in Poetic Passages

Formulating the theme of a poem is usually more complex. A biblical poem is typically a combination of ideas, images, and feelings. Given this multiplicity, it may be harder to decide what the passage is about and what it says about that subject.

Psalm 1 is a typical specimen. It begins with two verses that describe the activities that the godly person avoids and practices. This is followed by two verses of harvest images in which the godly person is compared to a productive tree and the wicked to chaff. Two concluding verses shift the focus to the future and predict judgment for the wicked and God's favor on the righteous.

What is the poem about? One good answer is to view the psalm as being about the godly person. The poem does not, of course, use that phrase. It is something we have to infer from the descriptions and images that make up the psalm. The specific theme is that the godly person is blessed. The poem itself describes in specific detail exactly how the godly person is blessed, partly in contrast to the judgment of the wicked. By itself, a general statement of theme does not do justice to the specifics of the text, but this can be accomplished in an actual study of the poem. The purpose of a thematic statement is to provide a conceptual unity within which to look at the specific details of a passage.

Thematic Unity in Narrative Passages

When we turn to the stories of the Bible, we may find it harder to formulate a statement of theme. While poems often share with expository discourse the tendency to state ideas, stories are different. They do not state ideas but instead tell us what characters in a given setting did. We then have to move from story to meaning, from event to theme.

The story of Peter's denial of Jesus (Luke 22:54–62) illustrates the difficulties that we may face with biblical narrative. The story itself tells what happens when Peter is questioned by three people around the fire. In keeping with the tendency of the stories of the Bible, the writer narrates but does not explain what happens. How, then, do we arrive at a thematic statement?

The best starting place is to identify the human experience that a story presents. In the case of Peter, that experience is a combination of temptation and denial. The story is a picture or anatomy of the ways that followers of Jesus can deny him. With this as the unifying focus of the story, we can begin to formulate subordinate generalizations: Christians can deny Jesus when they are put into situations that test their loyalty; when they are preoccupied with their own safety and become forgetful of their connection with Jesus; when they are fearful about what their identification with Jesus will cost them; when they think themselves invulnerable; and when they are caught off guard. If we are looking for a single statement of theme that will serve as an umbrella for these individual points, this will suffice: The circumstances of life produce occasions when Christians can easily and unknowingly deny Jesus.

Of course such a statement involves a certain reductionism. It is not an adequate substitute for the story itself, nor does it do justice to the subtlety of meaning that we should see in the story when we scrutinize the details more carefully. But this is not the purpose of a statement of theme. A generalization about the meaning of a story acts as a lens that brings the details of the story into focus. Without that lens, stories remain vaguely understood. Uninterpreted biblical narrative is a common failing of Bible teaching.

Practical Suggestions

The theme of a biblical passage must be stated in sufficiently broad terms that it covers the whole passage. Doing so usually requires a good deal of thought.

On the other hand, the statement of theme must deal adequately with the specifics of the text. To identify a passage as dealing with

Christian living or pleasing God or what God is like is probably to leave the passage at too high a level of abstraction.

Do not be timid in formulating the unifying idea of a passage simply because you do not feel like an expert. Stating the theme of a passage is part of the Bible teacher's task. Of course there is the possibility of a margin of error, but not to take the risk is to settle for ineffective teaching.

Stating the unifying theme of a passage is only the beginning of the process. When actually teaching the passage, one must organize the presentation or questions around the unifying theme. The statement of theme is not only a point of departure; it should be a continuous presence in the lesson.

Structural Unity

A second type of unity that is important in a biblical passage is structural unity. This refers to the way in which the passage is organized as it unfolds and as a whole. We have never adequately expressed the unity of a passage if we only state its big idea. We must also be able to show how the passage is actually unified by that idea in its successive parts.

Two principles underlie the structural unity of a passage. One is the principle of coherence—the way in which parts relate to each other, especially how one thing leads to the next. Another principle is the whole-part relationship in which parts relate to an overriding framework.

The structure of a passage must, moreover, be formulated in terms of the type or genre of the passage. The structure of a piece of expository prose, for example, is a flow of ideas—a conceptual structure. A poem consists of images and feelings much more than ideas. It is therefore much less likely to have the smooth logical flow of an expository passage. A story, meanwhile, consists of a flow of events.

Theme and Variation in Expository Prose

The framework that functions best for expository writing and poems is known as theme and variation. We have already discussed theme. Variations are the individual units by which a writer elaborates that theme.

The framework of theme and variation imposes a double obligation on the interpreter. One is to discern a principle that is big enough to cover the entire passage or poem. The second is to show how every individual item in the passage relates to the overriding theme. This, in fact, is an excellent analytic framework with which to teach a passage.

1 Corinthians 7:1–9 will illustrate how the framework of theme and variation allows us to talk about the unity of a prose passage. The subject of the passage is sex. Since the writer discusses both married and unmarried sexuality, it is necessary to state the theme in sufficiently general terms to cover both. The following formulation does so: God has made provision for people's sexual needs. With the unifying theme thus stated, we can proceed to note the variations on that theme which make up the passage.

The first variation is the idea that the single life is one of God's provisions for people: "It is good for a man not to marry" (v. 1 NIV). The next verse states the other half of the unifying theme, namely, that monogamous marriage is also God's provision for people: "but since there is so much immorality, each man should have his own wife, and each woman her own husband."

Having introduced the topic of sex in marriage, the writer proceeds to analyze it. One idea leads to the next by a process of logic. Having said that men and women should have their own spouse, the author next adds that spouses should meet each other's sexual needs: "The husband should fulfill his marital duty to his wife, and likewise the wife to her husband" (v. 3). The verse which follows fits into the ongoing flow of thought by explaining exactly how or why a married person should meet a spouse's sexual needs: "the wife's body does not belong to her alone but also to her husband. In the same way, the husband's body does not belong to him alone but also to his wife" (v. 4).

The next variation on the main theme adds to the progression of thought by underscoring how important it is that married people find sexual satisfaction in marriage and how easily sexual temptation will arise if they don't find such satisfaction: "Do not deprive each other except by mutual consent and for a time, so that you may devote yourselves to prayer. Then come together again so that Satan will not tempt you because of your lack of self-control" (v. 5).

The passage next elaborates the idea that God has provided both the single and married life for people: "I say this as a concession, not as a command. I wish that all men were as I am. But each man has his own gift from God; one has this gift, another has that" (vv. 6–7). The final variation on the theme that God has made provision for people's sexual needs is a restatement of the double emphasis of the entire passage: "Now to the unmarried and the widows I say: it is good for them to stay unmarried, as I am. But if they cannot control themselves, they should marry, for it is better to marry than to burn with passion" (vv. 8–9).

As this analysis shows, expository prose passages are organized on a principle of theme and variation. They are not random collections of discrete bits and pieces. They are woven into a coherent argument.

Practical Suggestions

It is not necessary to use the expression *theme and variation* when teaching a passage. The chief usefulness of the concept comes when a teacher is analyzing a passage in preparation for teaching it.

In inductive Bible studies, determining the structure of a passage is the responsibility of the leader. In general it is futile to think that a group can do a good job of determining the structure of a passage during a Bible study.

Structural Unity in Poems

The structural unity of poems is likewise a matter of theme and variation. The difference is that the variations on the main theme are not so consistently ideas as they are in passages of expository prose. They are more likely to be images or feelings than ideas, with the result that we must pay attention to the logic of the images and feelings as we divide a poem into its units.

To illustrate the usefulness of the framework of theme and variation, we can turn to Psalm 6, a lament psalm with such abrupt shifts that on a first reading we might wonder if the poem is unified. The unifying subject of all lament psalms is the poet's response to crisis. The unifying theme is that God can be trusted to help those in need. In effect, such poems show us the range of appropriate human responses to crisis.

The first variation on the theme of the speaker's distress in Psalm 6 is the cry to God for mercy: "O Lord, rebuke me not in thy anger, / nor chasten me in thy wrath" (v. 1). The second variation consists of the speaker's description of his crisis:

> Be gracious to me, O Lord, for I am languishing;
> O Lord, heal me, for my bones are troubled.
> My soul also is sorely troubled, [vv. 2–3a]

The speaker's third response to his crisis is to appeal directly to God for help:

> but thou, O Lord—how long?
> Turn, O Lord, save my life;
> deliver me for the sake of thy steadfast love. [vv. 3b–4]

To round out this movement of the psalm, the speaker offers a reason why God should deliver him: "For in death there is no remembrance of thee; / in Sheol who can give thee praise?" (v. 5).

The poet next pictures his personal feelings about his crisis in vivid detail:

> I am weary with my moaning;
>> every night I flood my bed with tears;
>> I drench my couch with my weeping.
> My eye wastes away because of grief,
>> it grows weak because of all my foes. [vv. 6–7]

Two final variations on the main theme of the speaker's response to his crisis shift the focus from a spirit of defeatism to confidence. First the speaker dismisses his enemies with a tone of assurance: "Depart from me, all you workers of evil; / for the Lord has heard the sound of my weeping" (v. 8). The final variation is the conventional statement of confidence in God:

> The Lord has heard my supplication;
>> the Lord accepts my prayer.
> All my enemies shall be ashamed and sorely troubled;
>> they shall turn back, and be put to shame in a moment.
>>>> [vv. 9–10]

Psalm 6 covers an immense range of emotional territory. In fact, the conventional lament psalm always includes a reversal or recantation: having declared his situation nearly hopeless, the poet ends with an assertion of confidence that God will deliver. But such apparently disjointed poems can be wrestled into a coherent whole if we apply the structural principle of theme and variation. In Psalm 6, every unit represents an aspect of the speaker's strategy for coping with his crisis.

Three additional aspects of the structure of a poem should be briefly noted. One is that most poems are built on a three-part structure consisting of an introduction to the subject, elaboration of that subject, and final note of resolution or closure. This is part of the shapeliness and wholeness of a lyric poem. The concluding note of resolution, we should add, might be of a very general nature (a brief prayer or wish is common in the Psalms), with the result that it cannot easily be regarded as a variation on the main theme.

A second principle that organizes most poems is contrast. In fact, a poem might be built around more than one contrast. Psalm 6, for example, will be more unified in our thinking if we acknowledge that it is built around conflicts between the speaker and his enemies, and between the speaker's inner fear and confidence in God.

Finally, many biblical poems use the catalogue or list as the main structural principle. Psalm 23, for example, catalogues the shepherd's acts of provision for his sheep. Psalm 121 lists God's acts of protection for the traveler.

Practical Suggestions

> The format of theme and variation is an analytic framework for talking about a poem. Far too much commentary on poems consists of nothing more than paraphrase (restating the content in one's own words). Stating how a unit in a poem contributes to the unifying theme at once allows one to make an analytic comment about the passage, and this is far more helpful than simply paraphrasing a passage.

> Compared with expository prose, a poem is a hybrid. The basis for separating material into a unit might be one of three things—idea, image, or feeling.

Narrative Structure

Narrative or story is emphatically not structured on the principle of theme and variation, though much Bible teaching and preaching tries to force it into such a mold. A story is first of all a series of events. Its structure is not a logical progression of ideas or a series of poetic images but a sequence of events. How, then, are stories organized?

The most universal organizing principle of narrative is *plot conflict*. The conflict may be physical, mental, moral, or spiritual. Characters in a story can be in conflict with other characters, with their natural environment, with supernatural forces, or with themselves. Stories may be constructed around more than one conflict.

It is impossible to overstate the importance of plot conflict as an organizing principle in stories. This is how most stories are structured. To try to make sense of the unity of a story without identifying the central conflict is to cut against the grain.

A second important principle is that stories unfold as *a sequence of episodes or scenes*. These are the separate building blocks out of which the storyteller constructs the story. One of the first things that we should do with a story, therefore, is to divide it into its constituent episodes or scenes. It might be useful to imagine oneself as a television cameraperson or play director.

A further thing to note about the sequence of episodes is that they unfold according to a principle of *cause and effect*. They are not randomly arranged pieces of information. They are a continuous sequence of events that produce a coherent whole. It is always relevant to show how an event in a story produces the next one, or how it is influenced by what has preceded. Together these events make up a shapely whole based on the structural principle of *beginning-middle-end*.

The structure of a story is thus far different from a journalistic account of the same event. In the journalistic account, the most important information is stated first, and then additional details accumulate in an order of decreasing importance. One or two paragraphs can be omitted without destroying the unity of the article. But a story recreates the chronological and logical order of events. Paragraphs cannot be rearranged or deleted without destroying the unity of the story.

Many stories are organized around a central literary *pattern*. Usually such a pattern is an archetype—a recurrent story pattern in literature. The most common ones are the quest, the journey, the death-rebirth motif, the initiation, tragedy (or the more specific pattern of the fall from innocence), the happy ending, crime and punishment, the temptation, and the rescue. The importance of identifying such patterns is that they allow us to see the story as a whole, not simply as a series of events that follow each other.

Since the structure of a story is more complex than that of a poem or expository passage, we might pause to summarize the things for which to look when analyzing the structure of a story:

1. Plot conflict(s).
2. A chronological series of episodes or scenes.
3. A complete action with a beginning, middle, and end, with the main events related to each other by a cause-and-effect relationship.
4. Story patterns.

To illustrate how these work, we have again selected the story of Peter's denial of Jesus (Luke 22:54–62) as a typical story. Verse 54 is an obvious beginning: "Then seizing [Jesus], they led him away and took him into the house of the high priest. Peter followed at a distance" (NIV). A script would state, "Enter Peter." The final verse is an obvious conclusion: "And he went outside and wept bitterly." Exit Peter.

The intervening verses move us from Peter's entrance to his exit and take us scene by scene through the crucial action. That progression, moreover, follows a common pattern in folk stories and is known as threefold repetition. In this pattern a common event happens three times, with a crucial change introduced the third time. In the story of Peter's denial the repetition has a cumulative effect, as Peter becomes increasingly desperate and outspoken.

The archetypal pattern around which we can organize the story is a combination of temptation, or test, and denial. As so often is the case in stories, the central character is placed in a situation that tests him. The elements in the sequence are three: the test of the hero's loyalty, denial as the response to the test, and the final outcome.

The story is also organized around plot conflicts. At the level of external action, the conflict is between Peter and three accusing characters. At the end, there is an implied rebuke by Jesus toward Peter. At a psychological level, we infer a conflict of allegiance or loyalty going on within Peter.

Practical Suggestions

It is impossible to discuss the structure of a story without using literary terminology. A story is not an essay. Its organizing principles are literary ones—plot conflict, a beginning-middle-end sequence of scenes or episodes, and archetypal plot patterns.

It is evident, therefore, that the process of formulating the structural unity of a story is even more multifaceted than was true for a poem.

7

Principles of Biblical Interpretation

Whenever we interact with a biblical text, we follow underlying rules or principles of interpretation. Usually we practice these rules without being conscious of them. The study of such principles of interpretation is known as hermeneutics. In this chapter we will discuss the most important principles of evangelical Protestant interpretation.

The list of principles is not something to be memorized. It serves more practical purposes than that. One of these purposes is to bring to consciousness things that good Bible teachers do intuitively but that they could do better if they were aware of the principles underlying their practice. A second function is to enlarge our range of interpretive tools, alerting us to things that we might otherwise overlook.

Furthermore, knowing the right principles of interpretation will spare a teacher from committing errors when interpreting the Bible. Often teachers commit such errors unwittingly, not realizing that their procedure violates established rules of interpretation. Finally, knowing the correct principles of interpretation will enable teachers to assess commentaries more accurately and critically than they would do otherwise.

We might note in this regard that principles of interpretation hang together as a system. A commentator who makes glib comments about Peter not being the author of the epistles ascribed to him will likely claim as well that Peter had naive views borrowed from Greek thought, that some of his views contradict other parts of the Bible, and that some of the statements in his epistles are unreliable.

We should realize that the principles of interpretation that we are about to outline are presuppositions with which we approach the biblical text. For the most part we cannot prove that these premises are accurate. They are the rules that evangelical Protestant interpreters have agreed are accurate. Other interpretive traditions obviously disagree with some of these principles.

The Purpose of Biblical Interpretation

Interpreters often operate on the premise that the purpose of studying and interpreting the Bible is to find *the* one right interpretation of a passage. This is indeed something for which we should strive, but it is not the chief purpose of biblical interpretation. The Bible itself states that goal:

> All Scripture is...useful for teaching, rebuking, correcting and training in righteousness, so that the man of God may be thoroughly equipped for every good work. [2 Tim. 3:16–17 NIV]

Our task in interpretation is not so much "to find the right interpretation" as it is to use the Bible for its intended purpose of Christian nurture.

Defining the purpose of biblical interpretation makes the study of the Bible more than an intellectual quest to find doctrinal truth. It focuses on the student's response. It also allows for a more relaxed approach to Bible study than often prevails. Scholarly disagreement about the details of a text should not blind us to the clarity of the Bible on the Christian essentials. Whenever people use the Bible for its intended purpose of spiritual and moral growth, they have achieved the main goal of Bible study.

The Nature of the Bible

Some rules of interpretation are comments on the nature of the Bible itself. One of these rules is to *operate on the premise that the Bible is God's revealed word, inspired by the Holy Spirit and therefore without error.* This is a foundational principle, and a great watershed between conservative and liberal interpretations of the Bible.

A number of important corollaries follow from the premise that the Bible is God's inspired revelation. Studying this book is obviously a serious matter. There is something personal about the text that we study, since God speaks to us through it. If the Bible is inspired by God, it is trustworthy and reliable. It will not mislead a person. This, in turn, implies that the Bible does not contradict itself. Being inspired by God, the Bible is more than an ordinary human book. It deserves a respect that we do not ordinarily assign to books. And because it is God's revelation to us, we can assume its clarity and authority.

This foundational principle is more than theoretical. It has practical implications the moment one starts to interact with the Bible. Acceptance or rejection of the principle will determine whether we are likely to go to the Bible in the first place. People outside the evangelical tradition are much less likely to adduce biblical data when they discuss issues of Christianity.

For people who accept this principle of interpretation, it may seem platitudinous and self-evident. But its importance becomes apparent the moment we read commentary that does not accept the principle. Then suddenly a belief in the inspiration and authority of the Bible seems revolutionary. Consider, for example, the following specimen statements that we culled from biblical commentaries:

> Many of the stories of the Bible are legendary, and critical scholarship has the task to expose this.

> There is an awkward contradiction in the text at this point. This suggests that there has been editorial activity here to reconcile the two versions that differed markedly from each other.

> The prophets speak the truth as powerfully as anyone has ever spoken it, daring even to put their truths into the mouth of God himself. "I hate, I despise your feasts," Amos has God say.

> Some of Scripture I must candidly say I find no less than abhorrent.

Each of these comments violates the principle stated above, and together they produce a far different handling of the Bible than when a person accepts the inspiration and authority of the Bible.

A second interpretive principle dealing with the nature of the Bible itself is to *assume that the biblical canon (the Bible as a whole) is an organic whole in which the parts fit together harmoniously.* Accordingly, one should interpret individual passages in an awareness of what is said elsewhere in the Bible. In the case of difficult or obscure passages, the interpreter should give precedence to biblical passages where the doctrine is clear.

The customary way of stating this principle is that Scripture is its own interpreter. The Reformers called it the analogy (correspondence) of faith, by which they meant that we should interpret a biblical passage in accord with the whole system of Christian doctrine. If Peter's comment that "the earth was formed out of water and by water" (2 Peter 3:5 NIV) seems obscure, we should interpret it in the light of what the Bible clearly teaches about God's creation of the world in Genesis 1 and elsewhere.

If the Bible is an organic whole, then the Bible in its entirety is the context and guide for understanding particular passages within it. For no other comparable book do we assume this kind of unity. Several customary procedures spring from the principle of the organic unity of the Bible. One is the modern practice of printing Bibles with cross-references. Another is the practice of gathering proof texts from various parts of the Bible to support a given idea.

To illustrate the usefulness of this principle, we can consider the visions of the four horses in Revelation 6:1–8. These verses are a pageant or procession of four horses with riders. The color of the horses is increasingly sinister, as we move from white to red to black to yellowish green. The various warriors carry such objects as swords and a pair of scales (symbolizing famine). What does this strange vision really predict? Exactly what Jesus predicted in a famous and clear passage in his Olivet Discourse: "You will hear of wars and rumors of wars. . . . Nation will rise against nation, and kingdom against kingdom. There will be famines and earthquakes in various places" (Matt. 24:6–7 NIV).

To believe that *the Bible as a whole is based on a principle of progressive revelation* follows naturally from what we have been saying. Written by numerous writers over a span of many centuries, the Bible displays change and progression in some of its ideas and practices. The most notable development is of course the progress from the Old Testament (Judaism) to the New Testament (Christianity).

An awareness of this element of progressive revelation has important applications. It will save us from trying to defend or follow Old Testament practices (such as animal sacrifices and other rituals) that were terminated in the New Testament age, and it will give us an adequate explanation for why we do not practice such rituals. The same principle will explain contradictions or discrepancies between Old and New Testament passages. In the Old Testament, for example, the concept of the afterlife is hazy, while in the New Testament it is clear and detailed.

With regard to the Bible as a whole, remember the following principles:

Assume that the Bible is God's trustworthy and authoritative revelation to you.

Operate on the premise that the Bible is a total unity in which the parts fit together harmoniously.

Be aware that the story and revelation of the Bible unfold in a progressive manner, with resultant changes and developments along the way.

The Language of the Bible

From the Bible as a whole we move to the rules of interpretation that concern the language of the Bible. We begin with the fact that the Bible is written in ordinary human language. The principle of interpretation that follows from this is that *the first step in understanding a biblical passage is to determine the straightforward, literal, or normal meanings of words, phrases, and sentences*. This sounds simplistic, but it, too, has far-reaching implications.

For one thing, this rule of interpretation prohibits doing such unnatural things with the words of the Bible as assigning mystical meanings to words and phrases. It prevents the interpreter from deciding that the words of the Bible are a secret code language, or from isolating phrases from their normal context in sentences.

In addition to prohibiting certain practices, the primacy of ordinary language in the Bible invites certain types of study. It encourages word study—inquiry into the specific meanings of words in their original language and context. It encourages scholars to explore the specific connotations and nuances of words, and teachers of the Bible to make use of these insights. Given the primacy of the normal meaning of words in the Bible, it becomes useful to know that when the psalmist says that God "searches" him (Ps. 139) he is using the word for winnowing.

> *The* problem of interpretation is the problem of re-creation. This principle is applied not only to history and music, but to everything else which requires explanation.
>
> Webster defines "re-creation" as "reanimation, the giving fresh life to something." To re-create the Scriptures, then, is to expound them in such a way as to cause the written word to become the living word.... Thus the process of re-creation involves such a complete identification of the interpreter with the authors of the Bible that he relives the experiences which were entailed in its writing. It means recapturing the attitudes, motives, thoughts, and emotions of its writers and of those concerning whom they wrote.
>
> Since the re-creation of Biblical literature is accomplished primarily through empathy, the use of the imagination becomes essential.... The imagination may supply the magic carpet which transports us to Biblical times....
>
> Robert A. Traina, *Methodical Bible Study* (Grand Rapids: Zondervan, 1985), pp. 93–94.

It is not easy to know how to state the principle that we must interpret the words of the Bible in their ordinary meaning. The usual formulation is that we must interpret the Bible literally, but this is misleading, since much of the Bible is figurative rather than literal in expression. The terms *normal* and *straightforward* are thus more accurate. Even when we use the word *literal*, we should do so with an awareness that we do not mean "literal rather than figurative," but rather "literal as opposed to allegorical or mystical."

This suggests our next principle: *Unless a passage declares itself to be allegorical in nature, do not allegorize biblical passages*. To allegorize means to translate the details of a passage into another set of meanings, usually a set of conceptual meanings. This principle asserts the need to interpret passages literally rather than allegorically; it does not question the need to interpret figurative statements in a nonliteral manner.

What this principle prohibits is allegorizing a passage, that is, translating the details into a set of conceptual or historical meanings that the text itself does not intend. This is not to deny that some passages in the Bible are intended to be interpreted allegorically. Jesus' Good Shepherd Discourse (John 10:1–18), for example, is an allegorical description of Jesus' redemptive life and death. But to *allegorize* means to attach meanings to a text in which the details were not intended to be translated into another set of meanings.

This practice, which supposedly had its heyday in the Catholic Middle Ages, actually continues to be one of the commonest features of commentary, teaching, and preaching in contemporary Protestantism. Here is a typical specimen:

> The story of David's picking up five smooth stones from the brook shows us how we can be of service to Christ. The fact that David *chose* the stones shows that Christ chooses us for his service. David's choosing *smooth* stones reminds us that Christ has to refine us and polish our rough edges before we can be useful to him. When we read that David chose five *small* stones, we see that Christ can use only humble people. The fact that David chose stones *from the brook* shows that we must be purified by Christ's blood before we can be used by him.

What is so bad about such allegorizing? It violates a number of foundational principles, including the intention of the writer, the normal conventions of language, what we know about literary genres (in this case narrative), the clarity of Scripture, and the relative objectivity of Scripture as a shared body of truth. Allegorizing is too arbitrary and subjective to be valid, and it removes the possibilities of controls on interpretation, since it allows a biblical text to mean anything that the ingenuity of an interpreter makes it mean.

In regard to the language of the Bible, follow these principles:

> First determine the straightforward, normal meaning of words, phrases, and sentences.
>
> Do not allegorize.

Rules for Individual Passages

When we narrow the scope from the Bible as a whole to individual passages, further principles guide us. The first in importance is this: *For every passage in the Bible, assume a conscious intention or purpose on the part of the writer, and the unity and coherence of the passage.* It is simply a helpful strategy to assume that the writer had a purpose in mind and that he worked out that purpose in a unified and coherent way.

Several corollaries follow from this principle. One is that it is possible to derive meaning from every biblical passage. No matter how difficult a passage may initially seem, we have a reason to attempt to master it. If we stare at a passage long enough, it will cease to be a bewildering collection of fragments. With enough patience, we can find patterns and connections within a passage. This same principle gives us a reason to harmonize details in a passage.

We must guard against claiming too much knowledge about a biblical writer's intention or purpose. In almost no instance do we have a statement by a biblical writer about what his purpose in a given passage was. The principle we are advocating is the more modest one of *inferred intention.* As readers, we look closely at a text and infer what the writer's purpose in the passage was. We have no privileged information, and we should guard against claiming undue authority when we use the concept of inferred intention in our teaching.

In appealing to the writer's intention or purpose, we are making a hypothesis. Its usefulness is tested by the amount of light it sheds on a passage and whether it is faithful to the text. Of course we make such inferences continuously as we read the Bible. We infer that the writer of Psalm 23 intends us to see a series of parallels between what a shepherd does for his sheep and God's provisions for people. We interpret the story of Abraham in light of our assumption that the writer told the story in order to offer us a model of faith to emulate. Often our conclusions about the intention of a writer are comments about what we know about the genre (type of writing) of the passage.

A second principle for interpreting individual passages is based on this very idea of genre: *interpret a passage in the light of what you know about its genre*. Every genre has its own conventions—its characteristic ways of operating. These, in turn, carry with them expectations and rules for interpretation. If a text is narrative in form, we know that we need to approach it in terms of setting, character, and plot. When we read a poem, we know that we have to divide the poem into theme and variation and to interpret figurative language.

The applications of this principle are extensive. We believe in the importance of the rule so strongly that we have devoted the entire third section of this book to it. Many of the things that Bible teachers substitute for interacting with a biblical text arise from their ignorance of literary genres. They allegorize stories and flit through parallel passages when discussing a psalm because they do not know what else to do with these genres.

Another rule for interpreting passages is to realize that *meaning is usually derived from literary wholes—whole books, whole chapters, whole paragraphs, whole stories, whole poems.* This is especially true for distinctly literary forms such as stories and poems. Except for such obviously self-contained units as proverbs (which are, however, usually arranged into bigger units), it is generally a liability to "think verses" when proceeding through a passage.

At the very least, the context of the whole unit will provide a richer or more specific content for individual parts. Often an individual statement in a passage, or an individual event in a story, will be nearly meaningless by itself. It may even assert something different from what the whole passage does.

The most frequent violation of this principle is a distressingly common practice of trying to get a separate theme out of every verse in a passage. The result is moralizing on the specific details of a passage. For example, in the story of the separation of Abraham and Lot (Gen. 13), we read that Abraham was very rich (v. 2). Commentators who are bent on getting a meaning out of every verse of the Bible begin to moralize about whether wealth is good or bad in this instance (Luther and Calvin came to opposite conclusions). But the detail about Abraham's wealth is not important in itself. It is part of the background information that explains how Abraham and Lot came to separate. In the total context of the story, the verse does not intend to make an independent comment about money.

The procedure of moralizing about individual verses breaks a passage into a series of fragments without a unifying focus. When we write a paragraph, we expect people to interpret it as a paragraph, not as a series of self-contained and unrelated sentences. We expect people to interpret our whole sentences, not individual phrases in them. The same principle applies to passages in the Bible.

A final rule of interpretation for dealing with individual passages is to *interpret passages in keeping with what you know about their context in the Bible.* That context is actually multiple: the immediately surrounding material, the book of the Bible in which the passage appears, the Testament (Old or New) in which it appears, and the Bible as a whole.

When analyzing individual passages in the Bible, take these steps:

Assume that the author had a conscious intention that he worked out in the passage and formulate what you think that intention was.

Stare at the passage until you can state its unifying focus and see its coherence.

Identify the genre of the passage and discuss it in terms of what you know about that genre.

Base statements of the theme of the passage on the whole passage instead of moralizing about individual details.

Place the passage into its surrounding context.

Interpreting a Text

We come, finally, to the procedures for actually interacting with a biblical text. We might begin by noting that *understanding a biblical passage involves two basic steps: observing or describing the passage as literally or factually as possible, and making more interpretive statements about the meaning of the passage.* At the descriptive level, an interpreter asks verifiable, yes-or-no questions of a text. Such statements must meet a standard of factual accuracy.

Interpretive statements are less objectively verifiable. Their value is judged not by strict and objective standards of accuracy but in terms of how much they illuminate or how well they explain or fit the details of a passage. Interpretive statements must, of course, be faithful to the text, but there is always a possibility that other viewpoints might be equally valid.

To say that the story of Abraham is structured as a quest story is a descriptive comment. To claim that Abraham's flaw through most of the story is his tendency to live by an ethic of expediency is a more interpretive statement. It is a factual observation that the parable of the good Samaritan is based on the narrative pattern of threefold repetition (in which a common event happens three times, with a crucial change introduced the third time). By contrast, an interpretive comment on the same parable is that the main purpose of this parable is to undermine conventional standards regarding who the good people of the world are.

A second procedure for interpreting the meaning of a passage is this: *first determine what the passage is about (the topic) and then analyze how the writer wishes us to view that topic (the perspective or theme).* For example, Psalm 23 is about God's providence. The specific assertion that the poem makes about that topic is that we can rest content in the sufficiency of God's providence, which extends to all areas of our need.

It should go without saying that we must allow a passage to set its own agenda of concerns. It is sometimes amazing to see what topic an interpreter links to a given passage in the Bible. The information that Abraham was rich (Gen. 13:2) led Luther to write seven pages of attack on Catholic monasticism, while the statement that Abraham built an altar to God (v. 4) resulted in several paragraphs on the need to have simple rather than elaborate church buildings. This is a classic case of bringing one's own agenda of interests to a text instead of letting the text set its own agenda of concerns.

A related principle is the need to *base interpretations of a passage on details that are relevant to the main concern of the passage, not on peripheral "stage props" in the passage.* By stage props we mean details that are part of the surface level of the passage—part of the overall situation—but not part of the intended message or theme. This rule is especially relevant to the stories of the Bible. In the story of Abraham and Lot's separation, the fact that the two principal characters were relatives does not mean that the story is about resolving family conflict. The relationship is simply one of the facts of the situation. In general, writers can be trusted to use devices of disclosure such as repetition and highlighting to signal what is of central importance in a text.

The man who studies theology . . . might watch carefully whether he increasingly does not think in the third rather than in the second person. You know what I mean by that. The transition from one to the other level of thought, from a personal relationship with God to a merely technical reference, usually is exactly synchronized with the moment I no longer can read the word of Holy Scripture as a word to me, but only as the object of exegetical endeavors. . . . Consider the first time someone spoke of God in the third person and therefore no longer with God but about God was the very moment when the question resounded, "Did God really say?" (cf. Genesis 3:1). This fact ought to make us think.

Helmut Thielecke, *A Little Exercise for Young Theologians* (Grand Rapids: Eerdmans, 1962), pp. 33–34.

When interpreting details in a passage, it is necessary to *determine whether a given detail is descriptive or prescriptive*—whether it is something that is only presented or described, or whether it is intended as something that the reader should follow or practice. Another way of saying this is that we must make a distinction between what the Bible records and what it approves. Often we need to go beyond the passage to other parts of the Bible in order to reach our verdict in the matter.

In stories, for example, we need to interpret whether a given action or character trait is merely recorded, whether it is a positive model to follow, or whether it is a negative example to avoid. When Esther enters the king's harem, she conceals the fact of her Jewish identity (Esther 2:10, 20). Is this recorded merely to explain how she came to be queen? Or does it imply that she compromised her religious principles by eating non-kosher food and participating in pagan practices in the harem? Or does it mean that she was an obedient niece? The interpreter has to choose from among such options.

The same need to distinguish between what is descriptive and prescriptive occurs in the proverbs of the Bible. When we read the proverb "be not righteous overmuch,...neither be a fool; why should you die before your time?" (Eccles. 7:16–17), we need to decide whether it is merely a description of how many people live, whether it is a piece of positive advice, or whether it describes an ethic of noninvolvement that we are meant to repudiate.

In reaching conclusions on this matter, we need to pay attention to the writer's implied or stated pattern of approval and disapproval. A particularly frivolous type of misinterpretation has arisen from time to time when interpreters have assumed that everything that a biblical hero is recorded as doing is somehow a positive model to follow. The truth is that the characters of the Bible, including the godly ones, are frequently portrayed as doing the wrong thing.

Another interpretive principle is that *the meaning of many biblical passages depends on, or is enhanced by, information about the original historical/cultural context that surrounds the passage.* In fact, details in a text often baffle us until we know the context to which they refer. In Psalm 23, for example, what kind of provision is pictured by the sheep's lying down in green pastures? What are the shepherd's rod and staff? What are the overflowing cup and oil with which a sheep's head is anointed? Unless we recover the details of shepherding from the poet's world, we will have a very vague understanding of the psalm.

When interpreting individual passages in the Bible, take care to:

- Differentiate in your own mind between descriptive and interpretive conclusions that you make about the text.

- First determine what the passage is about and then narrow the focus to what the passage says about that topic.

- Base your understanding of the theme of the passage on the central concern of the passage, not on peripheral details.

- Determine whether a piece of data is something that the writer merely records or observes, or whether it is a prescription that we are intended to follow.

- Do research to uncover the cultural or historical context to which details in a passage refer.

We need to approach the Bible with the right interpretive principles. These principles are not simply items to be memorized. They are tendencies that must become second nature to us.

Nor do we mean to imply that the interpretation of the Bible is rigidly systematic, as though we should mechanically sift every passage through a grid of interpretive principles. There is an art and informality, as well as a structure and method, to good Bible teaching. In fact, the prime prerequisites for interpreting a passage well will always be a keen eye for the obvious and a heavy dose of common sense.

8

Understanding the Methods of Inductive and Directed Bible Studies

Bible studies remain one of the most vital ingredients in the lives of many Christians from high schoolers through senior citizens. The quality of these study groups varies widely, of course. Where the quality is good, these studies contribute more to a person's grasp of the Bible than the Sunday sermon does. As authors of this book, we enthusiastically endorse the inductive and directed study of the Bible.

In this chapter and the one that follows, we describe a general approach to Bible study that can be used in personal and group study. Ours is a straightforward approach that focuses on how adults can carefully read and interpret the Bible. We do more than outline a set of "Bible-study skills." Our approach encourages people to apply their everyday skills in reading, observation, and analysis to the Bible. Our discussion will focus on the inductive approach, which forms the foundation of directed Bible studies as well.

What Is Inductive Bible Study?

In general terms, inductive Bible study falls within a broad category of approaches to teaching and interpretation that emphasize the process of careful and controlled *discovery*. Versions of inductive teaching are often found in schools under the label of "discovery learning" because careful, methodical, and intelligent discovery is the key to inductive study. Science labs, research projects, and class discussions are often designed to foster inductive or discovery learning.

Inductive methods place the burden for learning where it belongs—on the student. *All* learning is self-learning. No one can learn for someone else. In inductive approaches, the teacher facilitates and supports the learner's investigation and discovery. At their best, inductive studies work well because they implicitly acknowledge the fact that all true education is ultimately *self-education*.

Inductive Bible study is one way of studying the Bible in a small group. The methods used in small-group inductive study can, however, also be used in one's personal study of the Bible. There are seven distinguishing features of inductive Bible study.

Inductive Study Is Methodical

Good Bible study is always systematic and methodical. Unguided discussions about the Bible can be inefficient and disorganized, and are usually lacking in substance. They often focus on the controversial at the expense of the important. They are a law unto themselves and generally lack criteria by which to measure whether they are succeeding. We need an appropriate *method* to insure that a Bible study is truly a study and that it meets standards of excellence.

Yet many people recoil at the thought of applying a method to the Bible. It somehow seems stiff and mechanical. The fear is quite unfounded. We must study the Bible as diligently and in as informed a manner as we study any other important book. To say that the message of the Bible is contained in ordinary human language does not demean the Bible any more than acknowledging Christ's humanity demeans God. Like the incarnation, the Bible is God's Word in a human form. As long as we recognize that the Bible is God's Word and more than a human book, we need not fear that we will read it in the same mechanical way that we read an instruction manual.

Good Bible readers are something like detectives. They sift through the evidence in a systematic way before drawing a conclusion. We should not approach Scripture in a haphazard way, noting one fact, overlooking another, and rushing on to a predetermined conclusion. We should be thorough and careful in our study. Otherwise it is all too easy to read our prejudices into the Bible, or to rush to an interpretation that fails to capture the riches of a passage. Following a method is the only way to insure that we will be careful and thorough.

Inductive Study Uses
Careful Methods of Interpretation

Some people have complained that small-group Bible studies are no more than a pooling of ignorance and opinions. To these critics, inductive Bible studies are the perfect example of what the evangelist in Flannery O'Connor's story *Wise Blood* advocates: "You can sit at home and interpit your own Bible however you feel in your heart it ought to be interpited."[1] Unfortunately, such individualistic interpretation is the case in many small-group studies, but it need not be true for inductive Bible studies.

In inductive Bible studies the leader and the participants probe the meaning of a text in a careful and thorough manner. They give the biblical author the respect

1. Flannery O'Connor, *Three by Flannery O'Connor* (New York: New American Library, 1983), p. 78.

that they would expect in a conversation: they do not take what is said out of context, they take the words of the passage seriously, they avoid misquoting the author, and they consider the purpose of the communication.

Inductive Bible studies must meet the same criteria of interpretation that a pastor follows when he prepares the Sunday sermon in his study. Elsewhere in this book we explore what is meant by good principles of interpretation. Inductive Bible studies are not exempt from these rules of good interpretation.

Inductive Study Is a Shared Study

People can study the Bible any place or at any time, but there are many advantages to supplementing personal Bible study with small-group study. For one thing, many people find that meeting regularly with others for Bible study brings a consistency to their own personal study. In group study, moreover, people can use the other members to test their interpretations.

Even more important is the wealth of insights that come when a group stares together at a passage from the Bible. If group members are good at such staring, they uncover truths that all the commentaries a person will ever read on a given passage do not give. There is also the enrichment that comes from the different perspectives that group members bring to a study of the Bible.

The traditional pattern for many Bible studies had been for the "students" to learn from the "teacher." The leader was the expert. Possibly the leader would involve the student in discussion, but in the main he or she was the chief resource. This is what we might call "leader-student learning." Students learned from the leader.

In discovery Bible study we want to involve you in "student-team learning." While you may still have a *leader* to be your guide, your most significant learning will be from persons in your small group—from your team members.

Oletta Wald, *The Joy of Discovery* (Minneapolis: Augsburg, 1975), p. 9.

A group can also provide the support that is essential when people try to put into practice what they have learned from the Bible. Without mutual prayer and exhortation and the example of other group members, many people would be hard pressed to change the habits that prevent them from "living by the Book."

Because inductive Bible studies are shared by the entire group, they encourage discovery learning. There is a profound difference between simply being told something and discovering the same truth on one's own. Educational research has shown that discovered truth tends to be better understood, more meaningful, and less likely to be forgotten than "told truth."

Inductive Study Is Discussion-Oriented

Good inductive Bible study takes place in a small group that is not dominated by one person. It is a study in which all group members can share their ideas, ask questions, and seek help in clearing up confusions that they have about a passage. Discussion, brainstorming, and debating questions back and forth can all be part of an inductive Bible study. These are what make inductive studies the dynamic things that they are at their best.

The delight of a functioning small group is that it has one hundred percent participation. There is a commitment to group involvement before each person ever comes. This is not a spectator sport; everyone gets into the action. And participation means that individuals have the *joy of discovery*! A truth found for oneself is more one's own than a truth heard from someone else. Discovering it, opening your mouth and verbalizing it—in these acts truth becomes part of you.

Gladys Hunt, *You Can Start a Bible Study Group* (Wheaton: Harold Shaw, 1984), p. 27.

This is not to say that discussion itself is the *goal* of inductive Bible studies. The goal is human and social transformation. Discussion can be an important means to that end but is never an end in itself.

Inductive Study Is Scientific

When we say that inductive Bible study is scientific, we simply mean that it follows the order of the scientific method of inquiry. The scientific method begins with observation, not opinions. So does the inductive method of Bible study. The scientist forms a hypothesis that best explains an observation and then designs an experiment to test it. In a similar way, Bible-study members form an interpretation based on careful observations of a text and then test the validity of that interpretation with other members of the group. Like the scientific method, the inductive method seeks to base its interpretations (hypotheses) on careful observation of the Bible (data) and not merely on opinions and conjecture.

Of course there are ways in which Bible study is *not* like a scientific experiment. It is not scientific in the sense of being detached, impersonal, or mechanical. But this difference should not obscure the fact that a good inductive study shares with the scientific method the urge to test interpretations against verifiable data (in this case from the Bible) and not against prejudice or mere opinion.

Inductive Study Is Application-Oriented

Inductive Bible study is not just an academic or intellectual exercise. It provides an opportunity for the group members to see where they have excelled or failed, as measured by the Word of God. It also encourages people to see how they can put into practice what they have learned in the study. Here, too, the benefits of a whole group thinking together and drawing upon their diverse experiences have proven themselves over and over.

Inductive Study Focuses on Both Process and Product

In inductive Bible studies, both the process of study and its product are important. It is easy to think that the most important outcomes of a Bible study are the principles learned, the questions answered, and the understandings attained. These are important, but the very process of inductive study is itself beneficial.

In the process of the study, people encounter the biblical text in a deliberate and direct manner, thereby exposing themselves to the transforming power of Word and Spirit. They also encounter the personalities, experiences, and needs of other group members. Spiritual unity is one of the leading purposes of inductive Bible studies, though of course it comes as a byproduct of the study itself.

It is true, of course, that what is an unspeakable gift of God for the lonely individual is easily disregarded and trodden under foot by those who have the gift every day. It is easily forgotten that the fellowship of Christian brethren is a gift of grace, a gift of the Kingdom of God that any day may be taken from us, that the time that still separates us from utter loneliness may be brief indeed. Therefore, let him who until now has had the privilege of living a common Christian life with other Christians praise God's grace from the bottom of his heart. Let him thank God on his knees and declare: It is grace, nothing but grace, that we are allowed to live in community with Christian brethren.

Dietrich Bonhoeffer, *Life Together* (New York: Harper and Row, 1954), p. 20.

These are the distinguishing characteristics of a good inductive Bible study. It is important to remember that the inductive method is just one of several different ways to teach and study the Bible. Like all other approaches, it has strengths and weaknesses. A leader should understand these. The inductive method has proven itself over many years, but it should not be considered the best method for all situations, or appropriate for all biblical texts or all people.

The Methodology of Inductive Study

The heart of inductive Bible study is its method. Contrary to a popular misconception, not all small-group

Bible studies are inductive Bible studies. Inductive Bible studies will be small and will use discussion, but their hallmark is their method. The inductive method consists of three distinct steps or ingredients. They are observation or description, interpretation, and application. Each is designed to accomplish part of the process of understanding a Bible passage. When the inductive process is used in a small group, the leader asks the group members questions that cover these three areas.

Observation/Description: What Does the Text Say?

The first task of the group's study is to find out what the text says. This part of the process can be likened to a scientist making careful observations, or a detective looking for clues before drawing a conclusion. Inductive Bible study is built on the maxim that genius is 90 percent perspiration and 10 percent inspiration. Observation is often tedious and time-consuming, but it should not be bypassed in the hope that the text's meaning will become clear through a flash of insight. Without careful observation, there cannot be careful interpretation.

Systematic observation is the first and most basic phase in the actual practice of personal Bible study. Many times a person has a lot of trouble figuring out what a Bible passage *means* because he has not first done the work of carefully and objectively observing exactly what the passage *says*.

Ronald W. Leigh, *Direct Bible Discovery* (Nashville: Broadman, 1982), p. 59.

We should be on our guard against the "romantic" notion that the Holy Spirit can be trusted to illuminate by inspiration rather than by the teacher's diligent study. Study is the means by which the Holy Spirit ordinarily gives insights into the Bible. What the modern British poet Dylan Thomas said about the inspiration of the writer applies equally to Bible teachers: "The laziest workman receives the fewest impulses [inspirations]. And vice versa."[2]

Interpretation: What Does the Text Mean?

The next task is to ascertain what the passage means. Such interpretation extends all the way from drawing conclusions about local details in a passage to determining the main point of an entire passage. As an example of local interpretation, consider the first of Jesus' famous Beatitudes. It *says*, "Blessed are the poor in spirit" (Matt. 5:3). But what does this *mean*? To answer that question requires us to interpret. The best interpretation is that to be poor in spirit is to realize one's sinfulness and spiritual bankruptcy before God.

We must also interpret the meaning of passages as a whole. We usually do so in terms of what we infer the author's intention to have been. Applying this to the Beatitudes as a group, we might conclude that a main meaning of the passage is that followers of Christ are called to live by values that differ from those by which most people live and to order their lives by an unseen spiritual reality rather than by the promise of tangible earthly rewards.

The task of interpretation begins by attempting to ascertain what the passage *meant* to the original author and his audience. In other words, what was the author's message for his hearers or readers? The writer of Psalm 23, for example, talks about how God leads him "in paths of righteousness" (v. 3). What would an Old Testament believer have thought of when talking about God's guidance in right living? Primarily the law that was given through Moses.

But interpretation involves a second step as well. Because the Bible is the Christian's rule of faith and practice, we are interested not only in what the Bible meant but

2. Dylan Thomas, as quoted by John Ackerman, *Dylan Thomas: His Life and Work* (London: Oxford University Press, 1964), p. 123.

also in what it *means*. The task of the inductive Bible-study group at this point is to bring the original message of the text forward to our age and situation, without, of course, distorting the author's original meaning.

This is done through the identification of principles that faithfully summarize the author's meaning and yet speak clearly to today's church and society. To the writer of Psalm 23, God's "right paths" meant primarily the guidance of the law. To us it means more. It includes the entire Bible, the fullness of the Holy Spirit, and the teaching and example of Christ. We reach these interpretations by first identifying the underlying principle, in this case moral and spiritual guidance.

Application: How Can I
Practice the Truth of the Text?

At its best, an inductive Bible study should be practical and concrete. The principles found in a Bible passage are to be lived, not just known and believed. We all need help in translating principles into action. This is where the inductive study method again shows its strength. When people begin to draw upon their own experiences in life, we see applications that we miss when we are left to our own resources.

Inductive studies derive part of their power from their communal aspect. Through mutual example, prayer, exhortation, creative imagining, and critical reflection, participants encourage each other to see how the truth of a passage relates to life. They also motivate group members to act on what they understand.

Directed Bible Study

The title of this chapter promised that it would cover directed Bible study as well as inductive Bible study. It will not take long to fulfill that promise, because directed Bible studies are based on the same principles as inductive studies.

What Is the Directed Method?

Directed Bible study is based on the same methodology of observation-interpretation-application that we have outlined for inductive studies. How, then, does it differ from inductive study? It differs mainly in what happens during the actual study. A directed study replaces group discovery with the leader's sharing of his or her insights into a passage. Inductive study is radically democratic. It gives every member a vote. Directed study lets the leader do more of the talking.

We should not, however, drive a wedge too deeply between the two approaches. Even in an inductive study, the leader has the central role. It is a rare inductive study that does not mingle some comments by the leader with the answers that a group comes up with in response to the questions that the leader asks.

Conversely, in a good directed study, leaders do not do all the talking. They, too, ask questions that lead group members to discover the truth and contribute to the general fund of knowledge about the passage. It is only the *proportion* of leader's comment and group response that differs in the two approaches.

When to Use the Directed Method

We are convinced that the inductive method has many advantages for small-group Bible studies. But there are times when it should be modified. The inherent democracy of inductive Bible study can make it inadvisable for some groups. A class can also be too large to allow for the inductive method.

Sometimes the make-up of a group is wrong for an inductive study. For example, if a group has a large proportion of new Christians or high schoolers with limited Christian knowledge, teachers should probably take a more directed approach. Exuberance does not by itself make a person a good member of an inductive Bible study. People without much knowledge of the Bible or Christian doctrine often undermine the effectiveness of an inductive Bible study with their lack of knowledge or hesitancy to speak in front of people who "know so much."

Then, too, the clock often works against inductive Bible studies. It is difficult to conduct a good inductive Bible study in less than an hour. Unless the leader gives aggressive direction to the study, studies of less than an hour will regularly run out of time, neglect to make application, and produce frustration with the process.

Not all passages work equally well with the inductive approach. Passages that demand careful attention to background details pose difficulties for an inductive study. The Old Testament prophetic books are an obvious example. In the inductive approach it is difficult to use technical interpretive sources such as language reference works, historical research, or material found in Bible dictionaries. Another thing that is often slighted in inductive studies is the rich interpretive tradition of the Christian church as found in commentary by Christian scholars from the past and present. In short, it is easier for leaders to share the fruit of their study in directed Bible studies.

How to Lead a Directed Study

Instead of simply using a set of questions to lead a study, leaders of directed studies find it easier to work from an outline. An expository Bible study should reflect the structure of the passage. The main responsibility of the leader of a directed or expository Bible study is to "open the text" for a group, not to share personal opinions or even exhort people. It is natural, therefore, to let the teaching outline follow the flow of the text.

How does one come up with an outline? It is easy. The first step is to produce an outline that summarizes the organization of a passage, unit by unit. This outline should be detailed enough to account for every verse (though this does not mean that each verse requires a separate entry). The outline of the passage should contain only observations or descriptive information.

The second step is to expand the textual outline into a teaching outline. The list of things that one can add to the textual outline to make it a teaching outline is as follows:

Background information that helps to explain details in the text.

Interpretive statements that explain the meaning of details in the text.

Expository notes such as explanations, challenges, or expansions related to the text.

Questions. These are best placed at key interpretive points or places in the text that may not be as easily understood. It is always wise to include "understanding questions" that allow a leader to gauge whether students are getting the point.

Illustrations. Leaders of directed Bible studies should feel free to make points clear by illustrations drawn from their own life, from current events, from history, from their reading, and so forth.

Application questions. As in an inductive study, leaders should give group members an opportunity to apply Bible truths to their own lives.

The inductive approach excels at honoring the "priesthood of all believers." But it does not do as well at honoring the gift of teaching. We should heed R. C. Sproul's admonition that "though small groups and home Bible studies can be very effective in promoting renewal of the church and transformation of society, somewhere along the line people must receive educated teaching."[3] Directed Bible study allows people who are gifted and trained to teach the Bible to do so in an atmosphere that is conducive to their gifts and training.

3. R. C. Sproul, *Knowing Scripture* (Downers Grove: Inter-Varsity, 1977), p. 41.

9

Leading Inductive Bible Studies

Good Bible studies require effective leadership. For this reason, we will focus in this chapter on the techniques of leading a Bible study. Although we slant most of our remarks toward leading an inductive study, we would alert our readers that, with a few small adjustments, the same methods can be used in a directed Bible study. The leader of a directed Bible study does more of the talking, but the underlying principles remain the same.

Preparing to Lead an Inductive Study

The key to a good inductive Bible study is a prepared leader. Preparation must be methodical and thorough. In this section we outline the steps or ingredients that constitute such preparation.

Studying the Passage
Careful study of a Bible passage is the foundation of the inductive process. It begins with careful observation. To observe a passage, one has to stare at it. A good student of the Bible is never afraid of staring at the biblical text. Such staring takes time and mental alertness.

In this early stage of study, the leader's task is like that of a detective gathering information about a case. It is too early to know what piece of information might prove to be relevant. Any data about context, background, and specific details are welcome.

Prayer as Part of Preparation

Saturate your leadership ministry and your group members with prayer. It may sound oversimplified, but there is no substitute for persistent, faith-filled prayer. Pray for each member of the Bible study group by name often through the week. Pray for them as you frame each question or activity. Ask God to prepare them to participate and learn.

Ed Stewart and Nina M. Fishwick, *Group Talk* (Ventura, Calif.: Regal, 1986), p. 122.

At this stage the leader sets aside preconceived ideas about the passage. As much as possible, the leader tries to look at the passage as though it were the first time he or she had ever read it. The first task is to see the text as it is in itself. The description that C. S. Lewis gives of how to understand a painting is equally true of someone getting a grip on a passage from the Bible:

> We must look, and go on looking till we have certainly seen exactly what is there. We sit down before the picture in order to have something done to us, not that we may do things with it. The first demand any work of any art makes upon us is surrender. Look. Listen. Receive. Get yourself out of the way.[1]

The only qualification that we would make here is that a good reader does not forget the rules of interpretation while looking at a passage. For example, we need to observe a passage with an awareness of the kind of writing it is. If a passage is a story, we need to pay attention to setting, characters, and action.

1. C. S. Lewis, *An Experiment in Criticism* (Cambridge: Cambridge University Press, 1965), p. 19.

Tools of the Trade

The Bible teacher's preparation can be made far more efficient by the use of several tools of the trade. A small investment will provide the information and resources that can greatly enhance a lesson. Here are seven indispensable tools.

Study Bible. A good study Bible packs an enormous quantity of information into a single volume, including outlines of Bible books, introductions to books of the Bible, footnotes on important or difficult passages, a brief concordance, and maps. The *Life Application Bible* is especially helpful.

Concordance. A concordance provides an index to the Bible. It does this by listing the chapter and verse where various words occur, thereby allowing you to find a verse whose reference you have forgotten. It also allows you to find passages that address a specific topic or issue. It is advisable to buy a complete concordance that indexes all the words in the Bible, and one that is based on the translation you use.

Bible Dictionary. A good Bible dictionary will provide you with background information on biblical books and authors. It is an excellent resource to use when teaching the stories of the Bible because it fills in details about characters and settings, as well as providing information about specific books of the Bible.

Bible Atlas. Your teaching will be more effective if you can tie biblical events to a map. In most home Bible studies an atlas can be seen by all or passed around. For teaching a class, you might consider purchasing a set of maps in the form of overhead transparencies. An atlas like *The Moody Atlas of Bible Lands* by Barry J. Beitzel (1985), in which the maps depict specific events and are accompanied with color photographs, will be the most useful.

Bible Commentary. A one-volume (or multivolume) commentary on the Bible will often give helpful preliminary information on passages. We should note that because of their brevity, one-volume commentaries often leave important questions unanswered.

Bible Review. Although the scholarly bias of this bimonthly journal is liberal, we recommend it to discerning readers for three reasons: its articles simulate thought about specific biblical texts, characters, and themes, keep one abreast of current scholarly trends, and include paintings inspired by the biblical material covered in the articles. Address: P.O. Box 10105, Des Moines, Iowa 50340.

Books with Charts. Irving L. Jensen's surveys of the Old and New Testaments, as well as his study guides on individual books of the Bible, are especially rich sources of charts and diagrams. The Daily Walk Bible, published by Walk Through the Bible Ministries, also contains summaries and charts.

Good observation of a passage itself follows a discernible methodology. It begins with reading the passage several times. This reading can be enhanced if one reads the passage in several distinctly different translations. Translations can be grouped into families according to broad translation philosophies. The reader who chooses from several of these families will be rewarded with diversity.

Literal translations aim at accurate translation of words and often use the word order of the original language. Translations of this type include the New American Standard Bible (NASB), the Revised Standard Version (RSV), the King James Version (KJV), and the New King James Bible (NKJB).

Dynamic equivalent translations aim at accurate translation of words and phrases into precise equivalent expressions. For example, in the New International Version the Greek word for "flesh" (*sarx*) is often rendered "sinful nature" (twenty-five times). It was judged that "sinful nature" more accurately conveyed to the modern reader the author's intended meaning of *sarx* than did "flesh." The translations based on the theory of finding dynamic equivalents include the New International Version (NIV), Today's English Version (TEV), the New English Bible (NEB), and the Jerusalem Bible (JB).

Free translations aim at meaningful translation of ideas and concepts. Falling into this category are the Living Bible (LB) and J. B. Phillips's New Testament in Modern English (*Phillips*).

All three types can add to our understanding of a passage. The advantage of consulting a range of translations is that they often complement each other and yield more together than any one translation does by itself. In particular, one should note the unique expressions and differences among translations.

After getting a feel for the passage on the basis of his or her own observations, a leader will find it necessary to consult published resources on the passage. These include the notes in a study Bible, Bible commentaries on the passage, Bible-study aids, and perhaps reference books like Bible dictionaries.

Another step in getting a grip on a passage is to observe and note the important features of the passage. In the Sherlock Holmes detective stories, Holmes's attendant Dr. Watson says at one point, "You appeared to read a good deal upon her which was quite invisible to me." To which Sherlock Holmes replies, "Not invisible but un-noticed, Watson. You did not know where to look, and so you missed all that was important."

As we set out to observe a Bible text, we need to remember Holmes's admonition to dear Watson. Watson had failed to observe the important features of the client because he did not know where to look. Observation is a skill. Reading a passage fifteen times is no guarantee that the reader will observe everything of significance. To observe the significant aspects of the passage, one needs to know what to look for. Here are some aspects of a passage that the careful observer should note:

1. *The literary form of the passage.* For example, is the passage a poem, a story, or an epistle? Each one of these has its own set of procedures. Knowing this tells us at once what to look for in a passage.

2. *The structure or organization of the passage.* A passage will not make much sense until we grasp how it unfolds from beginning to end. An expository passage follows a flow of ideas. Poetry usually gives a series of images or emotions. In stories we should look for a flow of events.

3. *Repeated words, phrases, or ideas.* What words, phrases, or ideas appear repeatedly in the passage? We should not dismiss small words out of hand. For example, the fact that "in" appears twelve times (linked with "Christ" or an equivalent term) in Ephesians 1 turns out to be significant.

4. *Figurative expressions and other literary devices.* Figurative expressions need to be given special care. In the observation step they should be noted and examined.

5. *Connectives and linking words.* Pay close attention to the words *and, or, but, since,* and *therefore.* These words that connect sentences, clauses, phrases, and words work as the literary glue that holds the passage together. Their presence should be noted in the observation phase and further explained in the interpretation step.

6. *Contrasts and comparisons.* The practice of comparing or contrasting one thing to another is common in all kinds of writing. Furthermore, much figurative language involves contrasts and comparisons. Every comparison or contrast requires the interpreter to determine exactly *how* two things are similar or different.

7. *Time words.* Time words such as *after, before,* and *while* play an important role in narratives.
8. *Location or place.* These words are also especially important in narrative passages.
9. *Author and audience.* Understanding something about the author and audience can be essential to interpreting a passage. From the passage and reference works determine, if possible, who wrote the passage, details surrounding the writing of it, and the nature of its first audience.

Finding the Big Idea

Thorough observation of a passage should culminate in a statement of the big idea of the passage. This is comparable to a detective forming a hypothesis after he has sifted through the data. A hypothesis can always be revised if the need arises. But if a Bible-study leader has gathered sufficient data and stared at a passage long enough, he or she is in a position to formulate an accurate statement of the main idea of the passage.

This involves the two-step process that we elaborated in an earlier chapter. First we need to determine what the passage is about. Then we should decide how the writer of the passage wishes us to view that subject. The activities and questions in an inductive study should focus on what the teacher judges to be the central idea of the passage.

This does not necessarily contradict the discovery nature of inductive Bible study, though a leader often feels a certain tension between the desire to give a lesson the right focus and the wish to let the group discover the truth about the passage. It would be irresponsible not to take advantage of the leader's preparation. It is also unlikely that a teacher is in a position to abandon his or her own understanding of the central thrust of a passage on the spur of the moment, though some flexibility is surely possible.

Practical Suggestions

Studying a passage in preparation for leading a discussion of the passage is a process of discovery. This is part of the excitement of preparation. You do not have to know exactly where your study will eventually lead in order to get started. The right conclusions will emerge during the process of gathering data.

It is important to write down ideas as they come to you or as you run across them in your reading of study aids. You cannot trust your memory to retain all the data and insights that will eventually enter the questions that you ask. The best way to record insights, moreover, is on notecards, since these can be arranged in a meaningful order at a later stage.

Do not be worried about keeping observation, interpretation, and application in separate compartments at this stage. They will have to be identified later, but at this stage you are simply collecting the data that will later form the content of the lesson.

You will do yourself a favor if you photocopy the passages that you teach. This gives you space for marginal notes and allows you to underline or highlight parts of the passage with a sense of freedom.

Writing Questions: The Heart of the Inductive Method

Having studied a passage and determined its main idea, inductive study leaders must complete the process of preparation by writing the questions that they plan to use during the study. Questions are of three types—observation or description questions, interpretation questions, and application questions.

Creative and thought-provoking questions are central to inductive Bible study. These questions are used by the leader to foster group discovery and discussion. Good questions have at least six characteristics.

Qualities of Good Questions

Good questions are precise. Group members need to understand what is being asked. The goal is to get people to look for specific things in a passage.

Good questions focus on important issues. There are dozens of questions a leader could ask about a Bible passage, but not all of these would be relevant or important to a particular group. The most effective questions concentrate on the vital aspects of the passage.

Good questions have a purpose. Inductive Bible-study questions are not designed simply to get people talking. They guide people in their discovery of the Bible's message. Questions should be written to help accomplish one of the three steps of the inductive method (observation, interpretation, application), and they should in some way relate to the statement of topic and theme for the passage.

Good questions are thought-provoking. They make group members think and ponder the meaning of the text. Overly obvious questions waste people's time and bore them as well.

Good questions can be answered by the group. The leader should ask questions that group members can handle and that the passage actually allows them to answer. Teachers should try to make group members the experts by asking questions that relate to both the text and their experience.

Good questions are at least somewhat open-ended. They stimulate discussion and, unlike leading questions, they do not imply that there is a single correct answer. Leading questions beg for a particular answer, such as, Isn't Jesus the answer to life's problems? Usually these questions can be answered with a discussion-stifling yes or no. Leading questions can easily be changed into open-ended questions. Often simply adding a *why*, *how*, or *what* to the beginning of a question will transform it into an open-ended question.

In summary, we believe that good questions are precise (they can be easily understood); purposeful (they help to accomplish one of the three steps of inductive study and keep the discussion focused on the big idea of the passage); and productive (they stimulate both thought and discussion).

Observation/Description Questions

The challenge in writing observation questions is to make them interesting. It is easy to ask who? what? when? where? It is difficult to make such questions interesting and thought-provoking. Observation is a crucial step in inductive Bible study, but one that is too often hurried through because the members think the questions are simplistic. If the leader asks the straightforward, factual question, When did Nicodemus come to see Jesus? the group might think that the question is either insulting or a trick question.

At other times the questions are so technical that only the leader can answer them. For example, Where is Cenchrea? is a question that will not get many takers.

Either extreme stifles discussion and careful observation of the text. The goal of an observation question is to help people carefully observe the passage.

Practical Suggestions

> Remember that the *goal* of observation questions is to help people observe the passage clearly. Any question or group activity that achieves this goal is legitimate.

> If a question is overly obvious, leaders are better off stating the material themselves. Although inductive studies rely heavily on questions, they need not consist *only* of questions.

> Patterns of repetition are especially important in the Bible. Asking a group to find patterns or lists of things in a passage is often a productive observation activity.

> Remember, too, that the *process* of observation is as important as the group's answers to specific questions.

Four Types of Observation Questions

A set of good observation questions will look at the passage from a variety of angles. It is easy to achieve such variety of perspective if we are aware of the four types of observation questions.

Context questions. It is a central rule of interpretation that a passage must be interpreted in its context. To insure that this occurs in an inductive study, the group must take time to study the context. It is a leader's responsibility to ask questions or make background comments that place the passage being studied in relationship to the passages that come before and after it.

Background questions. These questions are concerned with the authorship of the passage, the nature of its audience, and its historical and cultural background. A lot of this material lies beyond a biblical passage and needs to be stated directly by the leader, but some details can be inferred from a passage itself. For many a passage in the Epistles, for example, we can ask questions like these: How does the writer describe himself in this passage?

What do you infer to be the situation in the church to whom this letter is addressed? What occasion gave rise to this passage?

Subject-matter questions. It is futile to discuss a passage without knowing precisely what it is about. Psalm 23 is about God's providence. 1 Corinthians 13 is about love. The parable of the good Samaritan is about neighborliness. Too often it is assumed that people know what a passage is about, but in fact this needs to be stated as clearly as possible.

Form questions. These are questions about the genre, organization, and structure of a passage. Knowing the genre of a passage (for example, lyric poem, story, theological exposition) at once tells us what we can expect to find in a passage. This needs to be established through either the leader's statement or questions. It is also possible to ask questions that will lead a group to explore the sequence of events or the development of the author's argument in a passage.

The form of a passage also includes literary devices like metaphor, simile, and rhetorical questions. While these usually require interpretation, they first require observation. It is therefore necessary to ask questions like these: To what does Paul compare the church in this passage? How many rhetorical questions does Jesus ask in this paragraph? What kind of statement is it when the psalmist says that he can defeat a whole army by himself?

Practical Suggestions

Observation questions must be short and clear. Class members should be able to remember them and should not have to ask for them to be repeated.

Observation questions should ask for a specific observation that can be tied to a detail in the text.

It is better to ask two short questions rather than one long one made up of several parts. In fact, avoid connectives like *and* or *but* in observation questions. Keep matters simple at this level.

Ask for factual observations rather than opinions.

Be sure that the questions relate to the main point of the passage.

Observation questions must be capable of being answered by group members on the basis of the assigned passage.

If possible, ask questions that will give several group members an opportunity to answer. For example, the question, "What do we learn about the character of Abraham in this event?" will probably yield multiple answers and perspectives.

Three Things to Avoid in Observation Questions

Do not use the first person pronoun (I, me, we) in observation questions. Such personal references should generally be saved for the application questions. At this point in the inductive process it is improper to assume that what was true for the first audience must be true for us as well. At this stage, it is better to ask what *the Ephesians* were called to than what *we* are called to, for example.

Avoid the excessive use of the interrogatives *who*, *what*, *when*, and *where*. Such questions soon become tedious.

In general, avoid beginning observation questions with *why*. Usually such questions belong in the category of interpretation rather than observation.

Interpretation Questions

The inductive method begins with observation, but it should never end there. The observation step provides the data for the interpretation and application steps. In fact, there is a logical sequence at work here: observation leads to interpretation, and the interpretive insights must then be applied to life.

To formulate good interpretation questions, we mainly have to realize how such questions differ from observation questions. Observation questions are designed to yield objectively verifiable answers on which people would agree. They must meet a true-or-false test of accuracy.

Interpretive statements about a passage are less objectively verifiable. Instead of being judged by a true-or-false test, interpretations are judged by more subjective criteria, such as whether they seem plausible, or the amount of light they shed on a text, or how much they seem to explain.

Interpretation always requires that we go beyond the surface facts of a Bible passage. It involves drawing conclusions based on the facts, or seeing connections between things, or seeing patterns into which details fall. Our understanding of a biblical text always depends on our going beyond observation to interpretation.

We should, incidentally, view observation and interpretation questions as existing on the same continuum. Some questions fall clearly into one of the categories. Others are closer to the middle, with the result that they simply *incline* more toward observation or interpretation.

There are no specific "rules" for writing good interpretation questions. What a leader mainly needs to do is simply develop the inclination to move beyond observation to interpretation. We must learn to look for the *significance* of the details in a text. With this in mind, we have simply paired some observation and interpretation questions based on two biblical passages.

Observation: To what does the poet compare the righteous person in Psalm 1:3?

Interpretation: How is the righteous person like a tree planted by streams of water? (The answers are multiple.)

Observation: According to Psalm 1:2, what positive acts characterize the godly person?

Interpretation: What does Psalm 1:2 mean when it says that the godly person meditates on God's law day and night?

Observation: In 1 Corinthians 12, what word patterns do we find?

Interpretation: Why was it necessary for Paul to emphasize the "sameness" of the Spirit to the Corinthians?

Observation: What metaphor does Paul use to describe the church?

Interpretation: How does the metaphor that compares the church to a body relate to Paul's main idea in 1 Corinthians 12?

Practical Suggestions

With the questions paired this way, it is easy to see that observation and interpretation go together in any adequate treatment of a biblical passage. The two types of questions should therefore be mingled together during the course of an actual Bible study.

For reasons that will be noted, it is important to have a nearly balanced number of the two types of questions.

Questions about topic and theme (the big idea) usually fall into the category of interpretation. Psalm 1 does not announce that it is about godliness and that the specific theme is the blessedness of the godly person. To reach this conclusion requires an interpretive leap on our part.

Inductive Bible studies (including published materials for studies) often avoid interpretation because it is potentially controversial. But the impact of the Bible on our thinking and living depends on our willingness to interpret its meaning.

Remember that interpretive questions are more open-ended than observation questions. They often have more than one good answer.

Elsewhere in this book we divide interpretation into the two categories of determining what something *meant* to the original writer or audience and what it *means* today in our own cultural setting. At many points it is important to be aware of this distinction. To insure that a group is adequately interpreting what a passage means *to them*, it is useful to ask a class to summarize the main teaching(s) of a passage or indicate the significance of the passage.

Another good strategy is to ask the class to compare something in a passage to a relevant modern-day concept. For example: A common sentiment today is, "If it doesn't hurt anyone, it's OK." How might Paul respond to this attitude?

Why It Is Important to Distinguish Between Observation and Interpretation

An observation is a comment about what the Bible says and how it says it. It is concerned with the explicit, the straightforward, and the factual. An interpretation is concerned with the meaning and significance of what has been observed.

There are several reasons why it is important to know the difference between observation and interpretation questions. For one thing, it allows us to gauge whether an inductive Bible study has adequate balance. Having too many observation questions results in the syndrome of uninterpreted biblical texts. Knowing the facts in a passage is never an adequate goal for Bible study. We also need to grasp the *significance* of those facts. The opposite abuse of too high a proportion of interpretive questions means that the study is doing too much interpretation on an inadequate basis. Meaning must be derived from a grasp of the details of a text.

Differentiating between observation and interpretation also tells a Bible-study leader how to deal with a given comment during a study. An observation must meet the test of accuracy. If someone comes up with a wrong answer to an observation question, a leader should challenge the answer. By contrast, interpretive statements are much less likely to have a single right answer. In such cases, a leader might wish to let an answer stand unchallenged even though he or she might disagree with it.

Finally, putting a question into the right category allows us to gauge how long a group is likely to spend on a given question. Observation questions usually do not take long. Interpretation questions ordinarily take a lot longer.

Practical Suggestions

Be clear in your own mind about which of your insights and questions are observations and which are interpretations. Sorting out genuine observations from interpretations is one of the tasks of a trial lawyer when cross-examining a witness. It is important for a Bible-study leader to keep in mind the differences between the descriptive (fact-oriented) act of observation and the explanatory (meaning-oriented) act of interpretation.

Even though interpretation questions are relatively open-ended, they must nevertheless be tied to the biblical text. Avoid questions that may have been *suggested by* something in the Bible but are not part of the meaning of the passage.

Although interpretation questions may have more than one good answer, they should ask for an interpretation of something *in the text* and should not simply ask for the opinions of members of the group.

Generally avoid the first person pronoun *we*, since this tends to draw people into application rather than interpretation.

Avoid opinion-poll questions. Your task is to seek the meaning of the passage, not group members' opinions about a subject.

Application Questions

The third ingredient in a good inductive Bible study is application to the lives of the members of the group. Here, too, it is possible to describe the methodology that one should follow in preparing to lead a study. That methodology begins by summarizing the main *principles* that have emerged from the observation and interpretation steps. Once the principles are clear, one can formulate questions that will lead group members to talk about ways in which those principles can be lived out in their own daily experiences.

One effective strategy for developing application questions breaks the application process into two distinct stages. The first stage, *general application*, essentially asks, "How are *we* going to apply God's Word to *our* lives?" The second stage, *personal application*, narrows and personalizes the process by asking, "How am I going to apply God's Word to *my* life?"[2]

In writing application questions, a leader can choose from several types:

Response questions. Evangelicals are rightly concerned about doing, but sometimes this concern can lead to a

2. Ed Stewart and Nina M. Fishwick, *Group Talk* (Ventura, Calif.: Regal, 1986), p. 47.

trivializing of a passage. Some passages call us to respond in deep and significant ways, but in ways that go far beyond the "What are you going to do *this* week?" type of question. Ask questions that focus on the response the author sought to evoke.

> The difference between the two stages of application is subtle but very important. At the first stage, each member is safely tucked within the anonymity of the group. The threat and commitment are at a minimum because each individual is only one of several discussing how "we" (our group, our church, Christians in general) need to respond to the Bible's message. The second stage brings each individual into the spotlight by asking, "How are *you* going to respond?" The generalities of a group response are good but each individual must make personal application of God's Word. Though there may be similarities in response between group members, personal application questions evoke the unique response which represents each person's unique relationship with God.
>
> Ed Stewart and Nina M. Fishwick, *Group Talk* (Ventura, Calif.: Regal, 1986), p. 47.

Bridge-building questions. Application completes the interpretive journey which begins by our entering the world of the text and ends with a return to our world. Application questions finish the process of bringing the text from the "then and there" to the "here and now." These questions ask, "Who are the Lots in our society?" "Who are the false prophets today who would assail Jeremiah?"

Situational questions. Here the participants are asked to relate the principle to a concrete situation. For example: If everyone in your family lived by this passage, how would things be different?

Practical Suggestions

Do not omit this part of a Bible study. Doing something is the goal of Bible study. Be sure to allow enough time for application.

If the application phase of an inductive Bible study is to succeed, the leader must take the lead in being open, vulnerable, and sincere in trying to put principles into practice in his or her own life.

Do not let the application phase become a detached discussion of ethical principles. Use projects, questions, and exercises to help the group members wrestle with the text's meaning for daily life.

Although observation and interpretation questions should be mingled throughout the study, it is customary to save the application questions for the end of a study.

Conducting an Inductive Bible Study

Thus far we have surveyed the steps involved in preparing to lead an inductive Bible study. The general outline of events is observation and study of the passage, stating the topic and theme of the passage, and formulating questions on the basis of the two previous steps. We now turn to actually conducting the Bible study.

Context and Background

It is a rare Bible study in which the leader can simply begin asking questions. It is much more likely that the leader will start by providing some kind of context for the group's study of the passage.

Often it is necessary to begin a Bible study with observation statements. Here the leader provides the group with important observations and background information that could not be found by the group on the basis of the passage itself. Of course the information should be limited to things that will enhance the group's study of the passage. Background material is not a time filler.

What things go into the opening comments by the leader? The range of possibilities includes comments about the author, cultural or historical context, type of writing (genre), structure or organization of the passage, and even topic and theme. By telling the group these things, leaders are spared from asking observation questions that only they can answer.

We should remember, however, that the key to inductive Bible study is discovery. It is preferable, therefore, to keep the opening statements to a bare minimum and to share only those things that would seriously hamper the effectiveness of the study if the group did not know them.

Approach Activities

An inductive Bible study need not be limited to questions and answers. Activities or exercises are also appropriate, especially as a way "into" a passage. We can call these "approach activities." Such an exercise or activity has as its goal getting group members to observe the text closely.

Observation activities coupled with observation questions are often more productive than just using questions. Sometimes they involve the entire group working together, while at other times it may be feasible to break the larger group into smaller units for individual projects. Here are a few activities that may lead to sustained observation of the text:

Charts. Group members graphically display different pieces of information with charts that show relationships or categories.

Lists. It is impressive how many things in Bible passages can be listed: repeated words or phrases, characters, places, writing devices like rhetorical questions or directly quoted speeches, and many others. Listing them makes them stand out in a person's awareness.

Scrambled passage. This consists of cutting a passage into sentences or phrases and having the group assemble the passage.

Sentence diagramming.

Outlining.

Guided reading. Each member or small group goes through a passage looking at an assigned feature of the passage.

Asking Questions

The heart of the inductive Bible study is the question–and–answer format. We have already stressed the need to prepare creative and thought-provoking questions. Their purpose is to allow a group to discover the truth about a Bible passage.

The discussion leader's role is to keep the discussion moving, encourage participation, and make sure everyone stays on the subject. Let's identify the components which fit together to make a successful discussion leader.

A catalyst. In Bible discussion, the leader is a catalyst causing interaction to take place among the discussion group members.

A guide. Whenever people participate in open discussion, the possibility of individuals getting off track and onto tangents is always present. The discussion leader must be a gentle but firm guide, keeping the discussion centered on the Bible text and discussion focus which have been selected.

A clarifier. Each individual who participates in Bible discussion speaks from his or her own background and frame of reference. And since backgrounds and points of view differ, someone in the discussion circle must clarify questions and comments so that each person has the maximum opportunity to understand what is being said.

An affirmer. A key element in the discussion leader's role is the ability to be an affirmer during the process of group discussion. An affirmer is one who encourages others by recognizing the value in each person and contribution.

Adapted from Ed Stewart and Nina M. Fishwick, *Group Talk* (Ventura, Calif.: Regal, 1986), pp. 25–27.

How leaders ask questions can be as important as what they ask. The question-asking process can be divided into three distinct steps:

Asking the question. At this point the leader needs to state the question clearly and communicate to the group that the question is worth answering. There may be occasions when a leader feels that a specific person could answer the question best. This can be communicated by eye contact or by direct question.

Waiting for an answer. Many leaders never give the group an opportunity to answer their questions. Waiting a few seconds for an answer is one of the simplest things a leader can do to increase effectiveness in questioning.

There is no reason to panic if a question is not answered immediately. In fact, it is amazing what can emerge if a leader takes a leisurely approach which conveys the impression that good answers are expected to emerge, no matter how long it takes.

Responding to an answer. The way a leader responds to questions will help set the tone of the study. The leader should seek to give undivided attention to the person answering a question. It is possible to demonstrate interest through such nonverbal listening behavior as leaning forward, nodding one's head, or simply looking interested. If a person's answer is unclear, a leader can help the person restate it in a clearer manner. Of course it is unfair and manipulative to restate an answer to make it fit what the leader wants to hear.

Handling the Wrong Answer

Sometimes it happens! Your Bible-study group is carefully looking over the text and responding thoughtfully to your questions with insightful answers that are right on target. Then suddenly, out of the blue, the "wrong answer" comes forth from an otherwise astute group member. What should you do?

First, remember that labeling an answer "wrong" involves a judgment call on your part. Don't be too quick to make that judgment. You might write off a genuine and unique insight as a wrong answer. Ponder the answer and see if it has more merit than you initially thought. Secondly, many wrong answers are relatively harmless and will be corrected by the better responses of other group members. Another possibility is to point out the error through one of the following appropriate strategies:

Ask the person who gave the answer to support it. In other words, considerately ask an appropriate version of the question, "Where did you find that in the text?" This works especially well with observation questions.

Invite other ideas from the group.

Ask a group member to assess the answer ("Tom, what do you think of that?"). It is of course unwise to play group members off against each other, but in a mature group this strategy can work well.

Give your opinion. Sometimes this is necessary, even though it runs the risk of minimizing the principle of group ownership of the Bible study.

Structuring the Study

A good Bible study does not meander. It has a sense of momentum and organization and movement toward a goal. Like a good story or essay, it has a discernible beginning, middle, and end. The leader is ultimately responsible to orchestrate the meeting in such a way as to achieve these qualities.

A simple principle to follow in this regard is to surround the actual study of the text with more general material. We might think of the study itself as a picture that is framed by other material. The logical beginning of a Bible study is some broad general statements or questions that give an overview of the passage. It might involve a question that asks the group to think about something outside the text itself. For example, in Psalm 73 the writer wrestles with the appeals of worldliness. It would be entirely appropriate to ask a question or two that gets the group thinking about that problem as they have dealt with it in their own experience as a framework for then looking at the psalm.

Once the study enters its middle phase, the leader needs to convey a sense of orderly progression. In almost every situation, the best way to achieve this is to begin at the beginning of the passage and progress through it unit by unit (though not necessarily verse by verse) in the order in which it unfolds. The one way to insure an unsuccessful Bible study is to jump from one part of the passage to another in disjointed fashion.

An additional rule to note here is that a good set of questions covers an *entire* passage. It is the leader's responsibility to make sure that there is at least one good question for every unit of the passage, even if a given unit is difficult to understand. It is better for a group to admit that they do not know what a passage means than to ignore it.

After the group has looked carefully at the details of a passage, it is wise to back off from the passage as a whole and ask some further overview questions that bring the whole passage into focus. A stock question along these lines is, What are the most important principles that we can learn from this passage?

Finally, after the passage has been explored and "framed," it needs to be applied. The most logical way to end a Bible study is with some form of application.

PART 3

The Bible We Teach

10

What Kind of Book Is the Bible?

How we teach the Bible depends partly on how we view the book that we teach. Some failures in Bible teaching stem from inadequate conceptions of the Bible itself. In this chapter we will survey some of the important characteristics of the Bible as a book. One of the important things that should emerge from our discussion is the idea that the Bible, for all its variety, is a unified whole.

A Collection of Books

The Bible is a collection or anthology of books. Even the word *Bible*, meaning "little books," suggests this. The Bible was written by numerous writers over a span of many centuries. Knowing this, we will not be overwhelmed by the sheer variety of forms and subjects that we find in the Bible. In its external form, the Bible resembles anthologies of English or American literature that we used in high school.

The fact that the Bible is a library of separate works results in a remarkable range of material and style. Within the covers of a single book we find virtually every

181

major type of writing—stories, poems, prose discourses, letters, visions, speeches, and much besides. We can see, therefore, how misleading and self-defeating it is to think of the Bible as consisting of a single type of writing. We need to be able to recognize the different types of writing that we find in the Bible and to apply the kinds of analysis that each type requires.

The Bible is a collection of interdependent parts. No single book of the Bible is totally self-contained. The meaning of individual parts is deepened and modified by other parts. Individual books or passages contribute their part to the total picture. Rarely do they say everything that we need to know about a given topic. The Song of Solomon, for example, does not give us a complete view of the Bible's teaching on romantic love. The Genesis account of creation is deepened and expanded by references to creation elsewhere in the Bible. In teaching individual parts of the Bible, therefore, we should be aware of what the Bible says elsewhere about a given subject.

Often one book or passage will be complemented by another part. Some passages emphasize God's sovereignty, other passages human choice. Sometimes our attention is focused on God's justice, while at other times we are asked to consider God's mercy. A lot of bad Bible teaching has occurred through the centuries when teachers have seized upon single passages as giving us the whole truth about a subject.

Another thing to note about this collection of books is that it is an ancient book. It comes to us from long ago. Its relevance extends to our own experiences of the moment, but we should not minimize the ways in which the Bible's world and customs are remote from our own. Instead of trying to obscure the differences between the two worlds, we need to begin by journeying to a world very different from our own. This is an obstacle to many young people and people unfamiliar with the Bible. Teachers of the Bible must acknowledge this potential problem and then devise ways to overcome it.

We should also note that the Bible is from start to finish a religious book. It exists to tell us about God. Human experience is constantly viewed in a religious and moral light. Part of this religious orientation is the tremendous sense of authority with which the Bible comes to us. It is not simply like other books that we read. Its claim to truth is overwhelming.

The Bible...is, through and through, a sacred book.... In most parts of the Bible everything is implicitly or explicitly introduced with "Thus saith the Lord." It is...not merely a sacred book but a book so remorselessly and continuously sacred that it does not invite, it excludes or repels, the merely aesthetic approach....It demands incessantly to be taken on its own terms....I predict that it will in the future be read, as it always has been read, almost exclusively by Christians.

C. S. Lewis, *The Literary Impact of the Authorized Version* (Philadelphia: Fortress, 1963), pp. 32–33.

To say that the Bible is a religious book and an authoritative source of truth is not to deny, of course, that it is also a very human book. From its pages we catch the voice of authentic human experience. It was written by and about people who tended sheep and spanked their children and baked bread. These same people were happy and frightened, sometimes filled with faith and at other times with doubt. To miss the human voice in the pages of the Bible is to teach the Bible as an emaciated book.

The Unity of the Bible

Along with the variety that we find in the collection of books that makes up the Bible, we find an amazing unity. We find a unity of national authorship, with only two books in the Bible (Luke and Acts) not having been written by Jews. The world in which we move as we read the Bible is consistently the Mediterranean world of Palestine, Egypt, Greece, and Rome.

The Bible also displays a unity of subject matter. We can describe that subject as God's dealings with people and the relationships of people to God and fellow humans. The character of God is a constant preoccupation. The nature of people is another. The unifying purpose of the Bible is to reveal God to people so they might know how to order their lives. Bible teaching should be oriented around such a purpose.

Theological Unity

The Bible is not organized like a theology book, but it embodies and teaches theological truth. That truth can be organized into a coherent system of theology. To attempt to teach individual parts of the Bible without fitting them into a theological framework is virtually to settle for teaching the parts of the Bible as a series of isolated fragments.

One of the standard categories of theology, for example, is the nature of God. There is hardly a passage in the whole Bible that does not tell us something about the character and acts of God. A useful framework for teaching the Bible is therefore the attributes of God. Complementing the attributes of God are his acts, which fall into such overriding categories as creation, providence, judgment, and salvation. Having such a framework in our minds programs how we approach passages in the Bible.

Creation is another main category of theology. The Bible expresses a complete view of the origin and nature of the world. God created the world in which we live good in principle. A permanent potential for corruption entered the world through the fall of the human race into sin. Even before the fall, moreover, the physical world was regarded as being of less worth and permanence than the eternal spiritual world. As the writers of the Bible talk about the nature of the world in which we live, therefore, they do so between the poles of affirmation and denial, hope and pessimism. We should approach passages in the

Bible with the expectation that they may say something important about the nature of the world in which we live, including the world of society.

The nature of people is likewise a unifying theological theme of the Bible. The Bible assumes a threefold view of people. They were created perfect by God and are therefore good in principle. They are evil by virtue of the general fall of the human race and their own wrong choices. But they are capable of redemption by God's grace. Beyond these general themes, the Bible asserts a host of further answers to the broad question, What are people like? Of special importance here is the biblical doctrine of sin, as well as of moral virtue and vice.

Another major theme of the Bible is the way of salvation, which focuses on the person and work of Christ. It encompasses ideas about the process by which a person can be saved from sin. Applied to the task of Bible teaching, we can say that many a passage in the Bible supplies answers to the question, How can a person be saved from sin and lead a righteous life?

The doctrine of the church also pervades the Bible. The question to keep in mind here is, What is the nature of the believing community? There is both continuity and change when we move from the Old Testament to the New. Concepts such as covenant and church are important.

A final standard category of theology is eschatology— the doctrine of the last things. Not every passage or book of the Bible contributes to the topic, but many passages do. As a result, we must be ready to ask, What does this passage tell us about the end of history and the life beyond?

In summary, an important part of the unity of the Bible is its theological unity. The Bible consistently gives us information about a set of topics and questions that together form a coherent framework of interrelated ideas. To see the unity of the Bible requires that we relate passages to this theological framework. At the same time, the framework gives us a set of questions to bring to passages that we teach.

Narrative Unity

In addition to theological unity, the Bible has the unity of a story. The Bible is above all a series of events, with interspersed passages that explain the meaning of those events. Equally important is the way in which the overall shape of the Bible is like a story. We begin the Bible at the beginning of history. We conclude it at the end. Between these is the unfolding of history through its phases.

This story has a unifying plot conflict. It consists of the great spiritual battle between good and evil. Virtually every chapter in the Bible contributes in some way to this conflict between good and evil. The presence of this conflict of course makes choice necessary, as the Bible concentrates on the person at the crossroads.

Every story has a central character around whom the action is built. In the Bible this character is God. He is the central actor whose presence unifies the story of universal history. The human characters in the story keep changing, but the central character remains constant.

The characterization of God may indeed be said to be the central literary concern of the Bible, and it is pursued from beginning to end, for the principal character, or actor, or protagonist of the Bible is God. Not even the most seemingly insignificant action in the Bible can be understood apart from the emerging characterization of the deity. With this great protagonist and his designs, all other characters and events interact.

Roland M. Frye, *The Bible: Selections from the King James Version for Study as Literature* (Boston: Houghton Mifflin, 1965), p. xvi.

The very arrangement of the Bible is loosely chronological, and in this, too, it resembles a story. We can make the outline of this story of salvation history either long or short, depending on how close we stand to the Bible. A happy median is the following outline of the story of the Bible, with each phase linked to the type of writing that we particularly associate with that phase:

1. The beginning of human history: creation, fall, and covenant (Genesis, the story of origins).
2. Exodus (law).
3. Israelite monarchy (psalms and wisdom literature).
4. Exile and return (prophecy).
5. The life of Christ (Gospel).
6. The beginnings of the Christian church (Acts and the Epistles).
7. Consummation of history (Apocalypse).

The literary form that welds all this together is of course history, and we should note that the concern with the events of history constitutes a further unifying thread in the Bible.

It is impossible to overemphasize the importance of this narrative framework as a unifying element in the Bible. Writers of the Bible constantly assume this order of events. They keep referring to the events that make up the story of the Bible and to its corresponding doctrines. The best evidence for this interlocking unity of the Bible is the modern study Bible with its cross-references. No other collection of separate books contains this degree of unity. As teachers of the Bible, we should approach individual passages in an awareness of the overall story that the Bible tells.

A Book of Encounter

Reading the Bible is not like reading other books. The Bible has a confrontational quality that makes it unique and that we need to acknowledge as we read and teach it.

Consider first the authority with which the Bible comes to us. The Bible itself constantly claims to be God's word to us. Its writers claim to be inspired by God. As a Jewish literary scholar puts it,

> The Bible's claim to truth is...tyrannical—it excludes all other claims. The world of the Scripture stories is not satisfied with claiming to be a historically true reality—it insists that it is the only real world.[1]

Throughout history the Bible has been accorded the status of an authoritative sacred book, and it is in this spirit that we approach it as readers and teachers. Studying the Bible is for Protestant Christians a sacrament—the means by which God is directly encountered and by which people open themselves to God's transforming power.

The element of encounter goes a long way toward explaining how the Bible affects us as we read and study it. The Bible is written in such a way as to make response almost inevitable. People either believe or reject what it says. The Bible awakens controversy in a way that most books do not. It presupposes response as a condition of reading. What Amos N. Wilder describes as an essential feature of the New Testament is equally true of the whole Bible: "It is as though God says to [people] one by one: 'Look me in the eye.'"[2]

One of the things that makes the Bible a confrontational book is its vivid consciousness of values. The conception of right and wrong is more sharply defined and more strongly advocated in the Bible than in ordinary books. Biblical authors are constantly saying, "This, not that." The Bible is similarly pervaded by the conviction that some things matter more than others. Ultimate value does not reside in anything or anyone apart from its

1. Erich Auerbach, *Mimesis: The Representation of Reality in Western Literature*, trans. Willard R. Trask (Princeton: Princeton University Press, 1953, 1968), pp. 14–15.

2. Amos N. Wilder, *Early Christian Rhetoric: The Language of the Gospel* (Cambridge: Harvard University Press, 1971), p. 54.

relationship to God. This preoccupation with values is of course something that needs to enter our teaching of the Bible.

From all that we have said, it is obvious that the Bible is a subversive book—a book that undermines and calls into question conventional attitudes and values. It challenges the way in which the human race has tended to order its affairs. In the face of a perennial human belief that people are basically good enough, the Bible hammers home the point that something is terribly wrong at the heart of human nature. Against the popular view that people should not be held responsible for their wrong actions, the Bible asserts that they are responsible. A question to have in the back of our minds as we teach passages from the Bible, therefore, is this: What conventional attitude or behavior that people commonly accept is challenged by this passage?

The power of the Bible to encounter people at the deepest level stems partly from its versatility—its ability to speak to every human temperament and faculty. At one level, the Bible speaks to our intellect and reason. It appeals to our grasp of the facts, both historical and theological. The Bible is in this sense a book of facts and ideas.

But the Bible is more than this. It is adept at imaging the truth—at giving us pictures of reality and truth. In addition to stating propositions, the Bible gives us examples in the form of stories about people. It supplies our imaginations with poetic images and with visions. The poet who wrote Psalm 19 assures us that the heavenly bodies, simply by virtue of their existence as physical phenomena, convey a message from God. The Bible often follows the same principle.

In addition to assimilating the truth of the Bible with our intellect and imagination, we experience the truth with our feelings. The Bible is an affective book. It moves us. And when we allow ourselves to be thus moved, we open ourselves to be changed by the Bible.

Now it is quite clear that the Bible authors often set out to instruct. It was not that truth did not matter; it mattered a great deal. But truth without life, knowing without doing, is a sterile product. . . . It is possible that parts of the Bible were not necessarily written to be taken apart and minutely analysed. They could have been written simply to have an impact on the hearer or the reader; they were written to stir the conscience and the reader; they were written to move men and women to action. If this is so, we shall not really understand such passages until we have been moved and stirred and stimulated ourselves.

John E. Balchin, *Understanding Scripture* (Downers Grove: Inter-Varsity, 1981), pp. 67–68.

To believe that the Bible speaks to us as whole people has a direct influence on how we teach the Bible. It affects how we approach individual passages in the Bible. If we think only in terms of propositional truth, for example, we will reduce passages to ideas and ignore the other ways in which a passage can speak to us. Our awareness that the Bible takes a multiple approach to truth also affects what passages we choose to teach. In fact, it will open us to the possibility of teaching the whole Bible.

11

Types of Writing in the Bible

One of the commonest misconceptions about the Bible is that it is all one type of writing. There are reasons for the misconception. The Bible is a religious book. It is an authority for belief. We tend to encounter the Bible in a religious atmosphere of devotional reading, sermons, and Bible studies.

All of these factors incline us to view the Bible as a single book and to obscure the variety that is present in the Bible. It is easy for us to begin to look upon the Bible as something that it is emphatically not—a theological outline with proof texts attached. As long as we regard the Bible this way, our teaching of it will be a continuous cutting against the grain. Any written document must be approached in terms of the kind of writing it is.

We also miss the rich variety of the Bible when we reduce it to just one kind of writing. The Bible is a book for all seasons. Sooner or later it appeals to every possible type of temperament. Within the covers of a single book we can find examples of a whole range of literary types—theological exposition, history, narrative, epic, tragedy, comedy, drama, lyric poetry, satire, love poetry, proverb, oratory, epistle, parable, and vision.

An Overview of Biblical Genres

The specific name for a type of writing is *genre*. Every genre has its own conventions and "rules" of composition. To interpret a text accurately and fully, we need to know what to expect of the genre to which it belongs. We should allow our awareness of genre to program how we read and teach a given biblical text. The purpose of this chapter is to describe the most general types that we find in the Bible. Subsequent chapters will narrow the focus to the subtypes.

The Mixture of Theology, History, and Literature

The Bible is unique among the great books of the world. Part of its uniqueness is the combination of ingredients that we find in its pages. We can discern three main impulses among biblical writers—theological, historical, and literary. Usually one of these dominates a given passage, but not necessarily to the exclusion of the others.

Theological writing in the Bible aims to convey general or propositional truth about God or morality. Here is a specimen:

> This righteousness from God comes through faith in Jesus Christ to all who believe. . . . all have sinned and fall short of the glory of God, and are justified freely by his grace through the redemption that came by Christ Jesus. God presented him as a sacrifice of atonement, through faith in his blood. He did this to demonstrate his justice. [Rom. 3:22–25 NIV]

Such writing states theological truth directly and propositionally. The only special skill that it requires of us is the ability to grasp theological or moral concepts. Since biblical theology makes up a coherent whole, passages of theological or moral teaching may also benefit from being related to other passages that deal with the same concept.

When we turn to the historical writing in the Bible, we are in a very different world. The historian's primary aim is not to teach religious concepts. It is instead the documentary impulse to record the facts about people and events, as the following specimen suggests:

> As for the other events of the reign of Joash, and all he did, are they not written in the book of the annals of the kings of Judah? His officials conspired against him and assassinated him at Beth Millo, on the road down to Silla. The officials who murdered him were Jozabad son of Shimeath and Jehozabad son of Shomer. [2 Kings 12:19–21 NIV]

The purpose of such historical writing is to record the facts. Sometimes the facts are placed in a moral framework of good and evil, and on other occasions they are put in a theological framework of God's providence in human affairs.

Purely historical writing poses special difficulties for the teacher of the Bible. To approach it as history means to be preoccupied with questions of accuracy and validation. But lay people simply lack the scholarly expertise to settle such questions. The most they can hope to do is parrot the information and opinions they get from the experts.

For all practical purposes, therefore, we should regard our acceptance of the historicity of the Bible as a presupposition, not as something we try to prove to a class. The history that is mingled with other types of writing in the Bible proves that the Bible is not a collection of fictional stories about God and people. The Bible records events that really happened, and this affects how we regard the Bible as a whole.

This is well illustrated by the account of a Wycliffe translator. After he had read the genealogy in the Gospel of Matthew to a group of Binumerians, one of the men raised his hand and exclaimed, "Listen, all you people! *This* is what we wanted to know. This is *it*! Is the Bible the white man's myths or legends, or did it actually happen? Now we *know* it happened. What myth or legend carefully records family names down through history?"[1]

While the historical thread in the Bible is thus important to how we view the Bible, most teaching situations allow little scope to approach it as history. But we should hasten to add that purely historical writing is a rarity in the Bible. The overwhelming amount of historical writing in the Bible is literary in form. That is, the writers go beyond the documentary impulse to record the bare facts. The writers usually present the facts in sufficient detail and concreteness to allow us to recreate the event in our imagination.

This brings us to the third type of writing in the Bible, the literary. Literature is first of all identifiable by its subject matter. The subject of literature is human experience. Literature aims to recreate an experience with enough vivid details that a reader can relive the experience. Literature does not primarily convey abstract facts but instead puts us through an experience. Since literature is more complex than other types of writing, we will devote a separate section of this chapter to it.

Expository and Literary Writing in the Bible

As different as the theological and historical writing in the Bible may seem, they fall into the category of expository writing. Expository writing is informational or explanatory writing. It is the kind of writing that we are taught to do in high school and college writing courses. We use expository discourse to conduct the practical business of daily living.

Expository language appeals primarily to our rational intellect. It aims to give us a grasp of the facts. Accordingly, it consists largely of propositional statements. It expresses the truth directly and requires a minimum of interpretation. Such writing is said to be referential: it

1. *In Other Words*, April/May 1983, p. 1.

exists to point beyond itself to a body of information. It performs this task best if it is a transparent medium that is itself invisible instead of calling attention to itself (see fig. 2). The more efficiently an expository text can point beyond itself, the better it has done its job.

Figure 2 How Expository Writing Communicates

Reader ⟶ Text ⟶ Information

Literature, by contrast, images the truth instead of discoursing about it abstractly and propositionally. We can thus speak of literature as appealing to our imagination (our image-perceiving capacity). The abstract intellect tells us propositionally, "You shall not murder." The imagination gives us that same truth in the story of Cain and Abel—a story that never even uses the abstract term *murder*. The Epistles describe the godly person with theological and moral abstractions. The poetic imagination of the Psalms images the godly person:

> He is like a tree
>   planted by streams of water,
>   that yields its fruit in its season,
>   and its leaf does not wither. [Ps. 1:3]

Modern research into how the human brain functions gives us a good framework for understanding how expository and literary writing differ from each other (and complement each other). That research has discovered that the two hemispheres of the brain are activated by different types of stimuli.[2]

The left side of the brain responds more actively to language and abstract concepts. It is active in analysis,

2. The literature on the subject of right brain/left brain is extensive. Two good summaries of research are Sid J. Segalowitz, *Two Sides of the Brain* (Englewood Cliffs, N. J.: Prentice-Hall, 1983); and Sally P. Springer and Georg Deutsch, *Left Brain, Right Brain*, rev. ed. (New York: W. H. Freeman and Company, 1985).

reason, and logic. In an experiment in which two groups of people were given lists of emotionally neutral and emotionally laden words, the people with the emotionally neutral words showed left-brain dominance in contrast to the other group.

We are far more image-making and image-using creatures than we usually think ourselves to be and...are guided and formed by images in our minds....Man...is a being who grasps and shapes reality...with the aid of great images, metaphors, and analogies.

H. Richard Niebuhr, *The Responsible Self* (New York: Harper and Row, 1963), pp. 151–52, 161.

The right hemisphere of the brain largely complements these functions. It responds to visual and other sensory stimuli and is active in seeing whole-part relationships. The right hemisphere is also more active than the left in the exercise of emotion and humor, and in grasping metaphors.

These descriptions of the two sides of the brain also describe the two main types of writing that we use and that we find in the Bible. Expository writing appeals to the left side of the brain. Literary writing is right-brain discourse. Effective teaching of the Bible requires that we respect the differences between these two types of discourse.

The Bible as Literature

The Bible is predominantly a right-brain book. When considered in terms of how the Bible presents its material, it more closely resembles an anthology of literature than a theology or history book. C. S. Lewis was correct when he wrote that there is a "sense in which the Bible, since it is after all literature, cannot properly be read except as literature; and the different parts of it as the different sorts of literature they are."[3]

We can safely say that at least three-fourths of the Bible is literary rather than expository in nature. It is appropriate, therefore, that we explore in some detail the neglected topic of what it means to say that much of the Bible is literature. Effective teaching of the Bible depends on our respecting the literary nature of what we teach.

Literature as Incarnation

Virtually the first thing to realize about literature is that it incarnates or embodies its meaning in the form of concrete images and examples. It images forth some aspect of reality or human experience. It gives us the example instead of the precept. Or, even if it includes the precept, the abstract proposition is never an adequate substitute for the work itself. It is only a lens through which we can see the experience more precisely.

This means that the truth or knowledge that a work of literature imparts consists of our living through of an experience. The corresponding activity that this requires of a reader or teacher is the ability to enter into the world of the text by means of the imagination.

The story of the fall of Adam and Eve (Gen. 3) provides a good illustration of the incarnational nature of literature. Nowhere in this text do we find a propositional statement of an idea. The story does not give us abstract truths but puts us through an experience as we accompany the characters in the story through a series of events. In fact, the theological terms that we use when interpreting this story are conspicuously absent from the text—the words *sin, fall,* and *disobedience.* Storytellers do not have a thesis to prove—they have a story to tell. They tell us about reality by means of setting, character, and action.

---

3. C. S. Lewis, *Reflections on the Psalms* (New York: Harcourt, Brace and World, 1958), p. 3.

In a similar way, poets (including those in the Bible)
speak a language of images rather than abstractions:

> He who dwells in the shelter of the Most High,
>   who abides in the shadow of the Almighty,
> will say to the Lord, "My refuge and my fortress;
>   my God, in whom I trust." [Ps. 91:1–2]

The poet here images the reality of God's trustworthy
protection. Our first task with such a passage is to picture
the images that the poet has put before us. The basic
principle of literary writing is that the author "shows
rather than tells," that is, embodies in concrete form
instead of abstract generalizations.

Because literature gives us the example rather than the
precept, it requires interpretation on the part of the reader
and teacher. In the story of the fall, for example, it is up to
us to draw the conclusions that the story is a picture of
sinfulness and the consequences of disobedience against
God, and of the cause and effects of guilt. Psalm 23 does
not explicitly state that the theme of the poem is the
security that comes when we rest in God's sufficient
provision. This is something we have to interpret for
ourselves.

Truthfulness to Reality and
Human Experience

We noted earlier that the subject of literature is human
experience rather than abstract thought. A story or poem
gives us an experience, not a set of facts or body of information. When we read a literary passage, we do not feel
primarily that we have been given new information. We
feel instead that we have been put in touch with reality.

This has important implications for how we view the
truth of the Bible. We have been conditioned to conceive
of truth largely in terms of an idea or proposition that is
true rather than false. But there is a whole other category
or type of truth—truthfulness to reality or human experi-

ence. We do not even have to state such truth in words. All we have to do is recognize it. We have grasped the truth of Jesus' parable of the good Samaritan if we recognize and respond to the neighborly behavior of the Samaritan.

> The rest of this book shall consider how the Bible, as literature, uses images in a great variety of ways. The stories, the parables, the sermons of the prophets, the reflections of the wise men, the pictures of the age to come, the interpretations of past events all tend to be expressed in images which arise out of experience. They do not often arise out of abstract technical language....We make decisions mostly on the basis of images....Our decisions are not made on facts; they are made on the way in which we see ourselves within the facts. This is "imaging." The literary author also uses images to represent the real crises in which we live....In reading the Bible you ought to begin by picturing what is going on. The genius of the people who wrote the Bible was to see concrete events and to picture them even when they seem to be talking to us in the propositional language of technicians.
>
> James A. Fischer, *How to Read the Bible* (Englewood Cliffs, N. J.: Prentice-Hall, 1981), pp. 39, 43.

Such recognition is all the easier when we read a literary text. Literature has an ability to capture universal human experience—what is true for all people at all times. Whereas a history book and newspaper tell us what *happened*, literature tells us what *happens*. This is the premise, we might note, of any good sermon or Bible study.

Based on what we have said, it is easy to see the corresponding activity that is required of us as readers and teachers of the Bible: we need to be able to recognize familiar human experience in the Bible. In Genesis 3, for example, we encounter a wealth of recognizable moral and psychological experience. It begins with temptation (vv. 1–5). When Eve longingly ponders the forbidden tree and comes up with three reasons why she should eat from it (v. 6), we can recognize the common experience of rationalizing a sinful choice. As the story continues to unfold, we find examples of shame and self-consciousness stemming from guilt (v. 7), fear of discovery and the impulse of the guilty person to hide from detection (vv. 8, 10), and evasion of responsibility when Adam tries to blame both God and Eve for his act of disobedience (v. 12).

Literature is life. The literary parts of the Bible are a mirror in which we see ourselves and our experiences. When we read and teach the Bible, we are in quest for more than the true ideas. There is a whole second type of truth in the Bible—truthfulness to reality.

Because the Bible is concerned to tell us not only what happened but also what continues to happen, we should state the truth of the Bible in terms of what it means to us today. We should state the truth of Genesis 3, for example, not only in terms of how sin happened to Adam and Eve but also how it happens to us. For us, too, sin occurs when we are tempted to sin by Satan's subtlety, when we unnecessarily prolong the occasion of temptation, when we disobey what God has commanded, when we allow ourselves to be deceived, and when we sinfully desire what God has forbidden.

Meaning Through Form

Literary writing often calls attention to itself in a way that expository writing does not. It requires that we analyze its form. In saying that, we should construe the concept of form very broadly as having to do with *how* the writer has expressed the content. Whatever meaning a text communicates is communicated through form, beginning with language itself.

This means that we cannot understand what a literary text says without first interacting with its form. Stories, for example, communicate their truth in the form of settings, characters, and events. To understand the meaning of a story therefore requires us first to pay attention to settings, characters, and events. Poetry conveys its meanings through images and figures of speech. It is therefore impossible to know what a poem says without doing justice to the images and figures of speech. We cannot assimilate and teach the truth of Psalm 23 without first talking about sheep and shepherds.

We should note in this regard that literature conveys its meanings by a certain indirection. The story of the fall in Genesis 3 simply tells us what the characters in the Garden said and did. On the basis of this we need to decide what the story means. Psalm 23 tells us about sheep and shepherds. We have to translate those facts into a human meaning.

To be preoccupied with questions of literary form is thus not a frivolous thing. It is a necessary step in biblical interpretation. We should not be afraid to talk about aspects of a text that seem far from anything "spiritual." We can trust literary texts to communicate their content by literary means. In fact, literary critics claim that the whole story or the whole poem is the meaning. Much of what a poem like Psalm 23 communicates is conveyed by subtle and indirect means as we simply interact with the sheep-shepherd metaphor. It is exactly these meanings that get shortchanged when we at once reduce a literary passage to a set of abstract propositions.

To talk as we have about the literary forms in the Bible is of course to raise the question of literary genres. Throughout the history of the world people have decided that certain genres of writing are literary, while others are expository. A propositional discourse such as we find in the Epistles is expository. Stories and poems are literary. So are the visions and dramatized dialogues that we find in such abundance in the Bible. To teach the Bible in keeping with the kind of book it is, we need to apply what we know about how literary genres work.

Every genre of writing carries its own expectations and conventional ways of communicating. One of the conventions of expository writing is that it progresses by paragraphs. The accompanying expectation that we should

have with such a passage is to "think paragraphs" as we
move through the passage. By contrast, the basic unit in a
story is the episode or scene, and that in poetry is the
image.

> The basic concern of this book is with the understanding of the different
> types of the literature (the *genres*) that make up the Bible. Although we do
> speak to other issues, this generic approach has controlled all that has
> been done. We affirm that there is a real difference between a psalm, on the
> one hand, and an epistle on the other. . . . These differences are vital and
> should affect both the way one reads them and how one is to understand
> their message for today.
>
> Gordon D. Fee and Douglas Stuart, *How to Read the Bible for All It's Worth* (Grand
> Rapids: Zondervan, 1982), pp. 11–12.

A final consideration that falls under the umbrella of
form in biblical literature is artistry and beauty of expression. The writer of Ecclesiastes tells us near the end of his
book that he arranged his proverbs "with great care" and
that he "sought to find pleasing words" (Eccles. 12:9–10).
The same claim can be made for the Bible as a whole. The
more literary the writer's form, the more artistry there is
to admire.

Whether this is something that a Bible teacher wishes
to talk about depends on the audience and occasion. Most
people are more interested in the skill of biblical writers
than we have been led to think. It is also a tremendous
asset to be able to show people that the Bible is an interesting rather than a dull book. The literary artistry of the
Bible is simply an added avenue to appreciating the book
that we teach and study.

Archetypes

We have noted that literature images reality in distinctly literary forms. A final identifying trait of literature underscores these tendencies. Literature expresses
its content in the form of master images known as literary
archetypes.

More specifically, an archetype can be either an image (light or bread, for example), a character type (the hero or the wanderer), or a plot pattern (the quest or the temptation). These archetypes recur throughout literature and life. They are the building blocks of the literary imagination.

> I mean by an archetype a symbol which connects one poem with another and thereby helps to unify and integrate our literary experience....Some symbols are images of things common to all men, and therefore have a communicable power which is potentially unlimited. Such symbols include those of food and drink, of the quest or journey, of light and darkness....
>
> Northrop Frye, *Anatomy of Criticism: Four Essays* (Princeton: Princeton University Press, 1957), pp. 99, 118.

When we read expository writing, we are rarely aware of such master images. With literature, we are constantly aware of them. Their presence is one of the tests by which we know whether a biblical text is literary and therefore subject to literary analysis.

Judged by this criterion, the story of Abraham's willingness to sacrifice his son Isaac (Gen. 22) is a literary text. The overarching archetype in the story is the test motif. As in most stories we have ever read, the hero finds himself in a situation that tests him. The journey toward a goal is also an archetype that organizes the story. Also important are the substitute and the pattern of encountering the divine on a mountaintop.

To see how archetypes function in poetry, we can turn to Psalm 23. The idealized pastoral figure of the good shepherd is one of the master images of literature. Sheep have similarly been idealized as images of innocence in the imagination of the human race. The archetype of the journey down a path, including passage through a low and dark valley, also organizes the details of the poem. Finally, many of the individual images in this

psalm are evocative archetypes of the imagination—
images of green pastures, still waters, a prepared table,
and an overflowing cup.

There are several reasons why it is essential to talk
about archetypes when teaching the Bible. They are organizing principles, both of individual passages and in the
Bible as a whole. Identifying them helps us to see the
unity of a story or poem or vision. It also allows us to
relate a given passage to similar passages within our repertoire, both within and beyond the Bible. Finally, naming
and exploring the archetypes in the Bible are good ave-
nues to sensing the universality of the Bible, since archetypes are universal symbols communicable to people of
all times and places.

How Literature Communicates

Earlier in this chapter we diagrammed the straightforward, referential way in which expository discourse communicates its meanings. To summarize what we have
said about the literary parts of the Bible, we can consider
how literature communicates (see fig. 3). Whereas an
expository text refers the reader beyond itself to a body of
information, a work of literature first seeks to encompass
the reader in a whole world of the imagination. It expects
the reader to share an experience, not simply to grasp a set
of ideas or facts. Only after entering this world and experiencing its qualities are we in a position to see beyond the
text to our own world of reality. We first look *at* the
world of the work and then we look *through* it to life as we
know it.

Figure 3 How Literary Writing Communicates

Reader ——————▶ World of the Text ——————▶ Experience

The potential liability of a literary text is that we have
to know how to enter its world. We have to know, for

example, how to interact with a story or poem. Because literature uses a technique of indirection and requires interpretation on the part of the reader, it is more liable to misinterpretation than an expository passage. By comparison, an expository passage is usually more accessible and requires no elaborate methods of interpretation.

But there is a corresponding liability involved in choosing an expository passage to teach to a class: because it states its content directly, it is quickly exhausted, and virtually the only thing left to do is apply it to real-life situations. By comparison, there is much more to do with a literary text. A story or poem has more density, more thickness, more experiential interest, than a one-dimensional, idea-oriented passage. A literary passage touches us at more different levels than abstract expository prose does.

We do not, of course, have to choose between the two types of passages. The Bible includes both. But we should remind ourselves that literary types of writing dominate the Bible by an overwhelming proportion.

The literary approach to the Bible is a rapidly expanding field. For helpful material on the theory underlying a literary approach, as well as explications of Bible passages, we recommend the following books by Leland Ryken: *How to Read the Bible as Literature* (Grand Rapids: Zondervan, 1984); *Words of Delight: A Literary Introduction to the Bible* (Grand Rapids: Baker, 1987); and *Words of Life: A Literary Introduction to the New Testament* (Grand Rapids: Baker, 1987).

12

Teaching the
Stories of the Bible

One of the most universal human impulses can be summed up in the four words, "Tell me a story." Not a day goes by without our telling and listening to "what happened," and explaining "what happened" is telling a story. The Bible implicitly obeys this human longing for narrative or story. In fact, narrative is the dominant form in the Bible as a whole.

The Challenge and Necessity
of Teaching the Stories of the Bible

Despite the appeal of stories and their prominence in the Bible, many people are afraid to teach them. For one thing, the world of the Bible's stories seems terribly remote from our own world. What are we supposed to do with all those battles and kings and weird names?

Teaching the stories of the Bible also requires that we know how to interact with stories as a literary form. In dealing with these passages, we need to talk about plot, characters, and setting. We have not been encouraged to talk about the Bible in these terms. In fact, we have so often seen the Bible treated as if it were a theological outline with proof texts attached that it initially seems "unspiritual" to talk about characterization and plot conflict instead of ideas.

And even people who are adept at talking about biblical stories as stories often find it difficult to move from the story to its meaning. They are good at assembling the specific facts in the story. They may even know a lot about the history. But moving from these facts to a meaning that we can apply to our own lives is formidable.

Despite the potential difficulties, however, there are several reasons why the stories of the Bible should figure prominently in any Bible teacher's repertoire. For one thing, narrative is the dominant form in the Bible. In terms of sheer space, the Bible contains more stories than any other form. Given this prominence of narrative in the Bible, any teacher committed to what the Bible itself calls "the whole counsel of God" can scarcely avoid teaching the stories of the Bible frequently. There is no excuse for Bible teachers and preachers gravitating so naturally to the most abstract and theological parts of the Bible, chiefly the Epistles.

The narrative mode is uniquely important in Christianity. . . . A Christian can confess his faith wherever he is . . . just by telling a story or a series of stories. It is through the Christian story that God speaks. . . . Perhaps the special character of the stories of the New Testament lies in the fact that they are not told for themselves, that they are not only about other people, but that they are always about us. They locate us in the very midst of the great story and plot of all time and space, and therefore relate us to the great dramatist and storyteller, God himself. The Scripture of Christianity is largely made up of narrative.

Amos N. Wilder, *Early Christian Rhetoric* (Cambridge: Harvard University Press, 1971), pp. 56–57.

Even apart from this obligation to teach the stories of the Bible, there are reasons why we should welcome opportunities to teach them. Stories do some things better than any other type of writing.

Stories bring us into an encounter with human personality and character. They are rich in human interest and recognizable human experience. Henry R. Luce, founder of *Time* magazine, once commented on his magazine's interest in personalities with the quip, *"Time* didn't start this emphasis on stories about people; the Bible did." It is generally much easier for people to see themselves and their experiences in the stories of the Bible than in other parts of the Bible.

Stories are also effective in transporting us from our own time and place to another world. We might call this their power of involving a reader in their action. In Bible studies this quickly focuses the attention of a class on the text. Stories create their own momentum by arousing curiosity about outcome. They also have a strong element of progression that keeps us moving through a passage. They possess the age-old appeal of "What happened? What happened next? How did it turn out?"

In short, a teacher's chances of success with the stories of the Bible are as high as they are with any other type of writing in the Bible. The purpose of this chapter is to note the general features of narrative as a biblical form and to explore the accompanying tools of description and interpretation that should govern how we teach a Bible story.

The Descriptive Level:
Setting, Characters, and Action

For purposes of illustration, we will keep our discussion of biblical narrative tied to a specimen biblical story, the story of Jesus' calming of a storm as told in Mark 4:35–41:

> [35]On that day, when evening had come, he said to them, "Let us go across to the other side." [36]And leaving the crowd, they took him with them, just as he was, in the boat. And other boats were with him. [37]And a great storm of wind arose, and the waves beat into the boat, so that the

boat was already filling. [38]But he was in the stern, asleep on the cushion; and they woke him and said to him, "Teacher, do you not care if we perish?" [39]And he awoke and rebuked the wind, and said to the sea, "Peace! Be still!" And the wind ceased, and there was a great calm. [40]He said to them, "Why are you afraid? Have you no faith?" [41]And they were filled with awe, and said to one another, "Who then is this, that even wind and sea obey him?"

Reliving an Experience

The first thing to notice about a story is that it does not consist of ideas (even though it embodies a meaning that can be stated in the form of ideas). A story consists of three basic elements: setting, characters, and action. In all three instances, we need to begin at the descriptive level, observing what we know about them literally and factually.

The purpose of a story is first of all to get us to share an experience with characters in the story. Stories, in fact, are filled with appeals to our imagination that allow us to recreate the settings and events as fully as possible. This affects how we should approach a story, whether in reading or teaching it. We need to be active as participants or spectators of the action.

> Narrative . . . draws the reader into the story as a participant. The reader is *there* . . . . The natural function of narrative is to help the reader hear the voices, take part in the action, get involved in the plot. We appreciate once again the significance of the realism of Mark's narratives, for it enables the reader to be caught up into the narrative as a participant.
>
> Norman Perrin, *The New Testament: An Introduction* (New York: Harcourt Brace Jovanovich, 1974), p. 165.

The power of a story such as the story of the crisis on the lake is its ability to involve us in what is happening. Before we interpret its meaning, we need to relive it. We need to be active in visualizing, in imagining scenes, in entering into the spirit of events, in identifying with characters. We should never be ashamed of staring at the concrete details in a story. After all, the writer placed them there for a purpose. If Mark thought it important that Jesus was asleep on a cushion, then it should be important for us.

Setting Setting is a good place to begin. It is first of all physical. This physical setting may add to the atmosphere of the story. Setting is also temporal. Furthermore, stories occur in an implied cultural setting with its own customs, practices, and beliefs.

Settings are important in stories chiefly in two ways. They are first of all part of the *action*. In fact, there is ordinarily a correspondence between a setting and the action and characters that exist within it. A setting is the fit container for the action and characters.

In the story of Jesus' calming of the storm, virtually every aspect of the setting helps to establish the danger that is the mainspring of the action. The physical setting—people in a small boat on a lake notorious for its quickly rising storms—is a picture of vulnerability. This setting creates an atmosphere of danger, with the temporal setting of nighttime darkness adding still more to this effect. The physical scene of waves filling a boat also contributes to the main action of this rescue story.

Often the setting in a biblical story is more than part of the action, taking on a symbolic value and thus becoming part of the *meaning* of the story. In the Old Testament story of Lot, for example, the wicked city of Sodom becomes a moral monstrosity—a symbol of materialism and sexual perversion. In the story of Jesus on the lake, the stormy seascape comes to represent danger and human helplessness. This danger, in turn, becomes a test of the disciples' faith. The setting is thus part of the very meaning of the story.

Practical Suggestions

> Be sure to do enough with setting in stories. It is often neglected, but it yields big payoffs when we analyze a story. In fact, the first descriptive question to ask of a story is, What do we know about the setting in which the action occurs, and how does the setting contribute to the story?
>
> The use of pictures, slides, or maps can add immeasurably to a class's grasp of the physical location of a story. Use whatever visual aids you can find to enhance your class's imagined picture of a story's setting.
>
> If you lack visual pictures, make use of verbal ones. Many commentaries contain helpful material, as do Bible dictionaries.
>
> Analyze the function of the settings in a story. How do they contribute to the action? How are they a fit container for (or extension of) the events and characters of the story? How do they contribute to the thematic meaning of the story?

Characters The characters are the second thing that we should note in a story. They are known to us in a variety of ways: by what the storyteller tells us about them, by other characters' responses to them, by their words and thoughts, by what they say about themselves, and above all by their actions.

In the story of the storm, for example, the disciples' fear and Jesus' calmness and power are evident to us by the characters' actions. We are made aware of these same traits by the recorded responses of Jesus and the disciples to each other at the end of the story (vv. 40–41). Earlier we catch the fear of the disciples in their accusing question to Jesus, "Do you not care if we perish?" (v. 38).

The only place in the story where the writer tells us anything directly about the characters is his statement that the disciples "were filled with awe" (v. 41). This is typical of the Bible, where storytellers generally tell us what happened but do not explain it. Storytellers in the Bible usually let the characters' actions do the talking.

Practical Suggestions

Look upon the characters in the stories of the Bible as real-life people and try to get your class to become acquainted with them as fully as possible. Ask yourself and your class, What do I know about the characters in this story? If possible, assemble character portraits on the basis of the details in the story.

The stories of the Bible tend to be told in a spare, unembellished style. This means that you will need to make the most of the few details that are given. Do not be timid in drawing inferences about characters in a Bible story. This is part of the task of interpretation.

The characters of the Bible tend to be universal types. We have met them elsewhere in our own experience. Explore this universal dimension of the characters portrayed in the Bible. Be creative in imagining the modern-day counterparts to biblical characters wherever appropriate.

Action or Plot The third main ingredient in a story is the plot or action, and this is somewhat more complex than considerations of setting and characterization. To begin, stories are structured on a principle of beginning-middle-end. This shapeliness is what makes a story a whole or complete action.

A story differs in this regard from journalistic reportage, where a summary of the most important information appears first, with other details added on the principle of accumulation. A story is structured in such a way to take us through the action in the order in which it unfolds. We cannot simply rearrange the details in a story the way we can in a newspaper article. At a descriptive level, it is absolutely essential to pay attention to what literally happens as the action unfolds and to lay out the action in its successive phases.

Just as important is the principle of plot conflict. Nearly every story is built around one or more conflicts moving toward a resolution. This is simply how stories are told. It is therefore always appropriate to identify the plot conflict(s) of a story. Story conflicts can be physical conflicts, conflicts between characters, or moral/spiritual conflicts.

In the story that we have been considering, the main physical conflict is between the disciples and the storm that threatens their lives. This, in turn, produces a character clash between the disciples and Jesus. At a more interpretive level, we can sense a conflict within the disciples between fear and faith. Talking about conflicts in a story may seem remote from anything "spiritual," but we cannot overemphasize how self-defeating it is to try to do justice to a Bible story without acknowledging that this is how stories are structured.

In the conflict around which a story is built, the central character is called the protagonist. The forces arrayed against the protagonist are called the antagonists. The importance of this concept is that we go through the action from the viewpoint of the protagonist (literally, "the first struggler"). We identify most strongly with the protagonist and view him or her as our representative. In the storm at sea, we go through the event from the viewpoint of the disciples. In their responses we see ourselves.

One of the commonest storytelling strategies is to picture characters in situations that *test* them. The tests might be tests of physical strength or resourcefulness, mental or psychological tests, or moral/spiritual tests. The element of testing in stories is often related to the motif of *choice*. Identifying the nature of the test or choice is not only useful as an organizing framework; it is usually a key to the story's meaning. In the present instance, we end the story with the impression that the test of the disciples' courage and composure has also been a test of their faith in Jesus.

Practical Suggestions

When teaching the stories of the Bible, do not neglect to answer the obvious question, What happens during the course of the story? Do not assume that class members have a grasp of the action. You will often be surprised by how much people have missed.

Be sure to divide a story into its progressive units or episodes. It is often helpful to view a story as though it were a play and arrange it into successive scenes. Be sure to identify the characters and setting for each scene.

Take time to determine the plot conflict(s) around which a story is built. This takes some analytic thought, but it pays big dividends in allowing you to see how a story is structured. Also note how conflicts are resolved at the end of the story.

Stories are usually constructed around the testing and choice of characters. Wherever these appear, identify them.

In all of the above considerations, tie the action of the story into your final understanding of the *meaning* of the story.

From Story to Meaning

What we have said about stories thus far has mainly concerned descriptive questions about what happens, where it happens, and to whom it happens. But stories require us to interpret their meaning as well as describe their surface details. Stories are implied comments about life. We should read them with the assumption that they make a significant statement about God, people, or reality.

> The whole story is the meaning, because it is an experience, not an abstraction.... The writer... makes his statements by selection, and if he is any good, he selects every word for a reason, every detail for a reason, every incident for a reason, and arranges them in a certain time-sequence for a reason.... When you write [a story] you are speaking *with* character and action, not *about* character and action.
>
> Flannery O'Connor, *Mystery and Manners*, ed. Sally and Robert Fitzgerald (New York: Farrar, Straus & Giroux, 1957), pp. 73, 75–76.

Stories, of course, make these assertions *indirectly*. They tell us about God and life *by means of* setting, characters, and action. They embody or incarnate meaning in a concrete form. They give the example and ask us to come up with the precept. There is a discursive level to stories, meaning that the storyteller is telling the story as a way of communicating truth to the reader or listener.

In stories, this meaning is always tied to the characters in the story. Characters in a story carry a burden of meaning larger than themselves. They become our representatives. What happens to them is in some sense a comment about life in general. We should, moreover, look upon characters in stories as people who undertake an experiment in living. The outcome of their experiment is an implied comment on its adequacy or inadequacy. We should note in this regard that stories might embody a positive truth by negative example. They often show us what to do by portraying a character who failed to do it.

As we move from description to interpretation, it is useful to divide the task into two phases. One is to decide *what the story is about*. The second is to determine *how the story asks us to view the experience that is portrayed*.

What a Story Is About

Storytellers use several devices of disclosure to signal what the action is about. One is repetition. Another is highlighting. The amount of space given to a character or event (the rule of proportionate space) is also a clue to what is important in a story. Even when a detail in a story gets little space, if it is the crucial or decisive detail it can be trusted to point toward what is central in the story's meaning. Finally, the safest guide of all when we determine what a story is about is to summarize what happens in the story. Another way to say this is that every story is in some sense an *example story*. We should therefore ask what the story is an example *of*.

In the story of Jesus' calming of the waves, these devices of disclosure point toward two main concerns. One focus of the story from beginning to end is the character or identity of Jesus. We can therefore infer that the writer intended the story to tell us something important about who Jesus is. But since equal space is devoted to the responses of the disciples to their crisis, we can also infer that the story is intended as a comment about human fear. The question, "What happens in this story?" points in the same two directions: in this story, Jesus shows his power over nature and the disciples respond to a crisis with fear.

Point of View

Once we have discovered what a biblical story is about (and it might be about more than one thing), we need to complete the task of interpretation by determining exactly what the storyteller says about and with that subject matter. What perspective are we invited to share with the writer? The common term for this is *point of view* in a story.

The most elemental form of narrative interpretation is "choosing sides." As we read a story, we are continuously called to make decisions about whether a given character or event is good or bad, sympathetic or unsympathetic. A carefully told story is a system of controls in which the writer influences our pattern of approval and disapproval. Stories are *affective* by their nature. They draw us into an encounter with characters and events to which we inevitably respond. Responses can, of course, be wrong, but we will do a better job of interpreting the stories of the Bible if we pay attention to our approval pattern.

All writers have, and must have, to compose any kind of story, some picture of the world, and of what is right and wrong in that world. . . . For a reader must never be left in doubt about the meaning of a story.

Joyce Cary, *Art and Reality* (Garden City, N.Y.: Doubleday, 1961), pp. 174, 132.

Sometimes a biblical storyteller enters the story and directly states an interpretive framework for the story. But such authorial statement is extremely rare in the Bible, and it is absent from the story at which we have been looking.

Instead of the writer's stating the meaning of a story, we sometimes encounter statements by characters in a story that illuminate the meaning of the story. In the story of the calming of the sea, the final verse illustrates this strategy. Jesus asks the disciples, "Why are you afraid? Have you no faith?" This influences how we interpret the disciples' earlier fear. In fact, each question is important here. The first is a rebuke and implies that the disciples should not have been terrified. The second question influences us to view the fear as a lapse of faith.

In the same verse, the disciples, too, ask a question: "Who then is this, that even wind and sea obey him?" The disciples here become our representatives. They raise the question of Jesus' identity and thereby push us to interpret the story as a comment about who Jesus is.

In addition to commentary by the storyteller or statements by characters in the story, the principle of selectivity and arrangement of material influences how we interpret a story. Storytellers control what we see and don't see. The story we have been considering has a far different impact on us because the writer included the rebuke of Jesus. The storyteller goes out of his way, moreover, to contrast the terror of the storm and the calmness of Jesus. Almost everything in the story heightens the power of Jesus over nature. The deity of Jesus stands silhouetted in the story through the way the writer conducts the description of the event.

The way in which a story ends can be a crucial factor in letting us know how the writer intends us to interpret the action that has preceded. After all, the outcome of a character's experiment in living is an implied comment on whether it was good or bad. In the story we have been considering, the final verse casts a retrospective glance over the story and suggests an interpretation of the action. Jesus' accusing question, "Have you no faith?" alerts us that the disciples' fear has been a spiritual lapse as well as a psychological terror. And the very last detail that the writer includes suggests an interpretation of the other main concern of the story, the identity of Jesus: "Who then is this, that even wind and sea obey him?"

To move from story to meaning involves a risk. A story does not state what it is about and how we are intended to view that subject. There is always the possibility that people will see things differently. We are rather constantly aware of a possible margin of error.

We should, however, accept the interpretive challenge with confidence. Knowing that stories are *examples* of something, we can follow the clues laid down by the writer's devices of disclosure to determine what the story says about life and truth by means of setting, characters, and action.

Practical Suggestions

Do not avoid interpreting the meaning of a story simply because you feel like less than an expert on the matter. Uninterpreted biblical narrative—simply reliving the story and stopping at that point—is a great waste of effort. The Bible is a book that tells us how to live, and it is our task to interpret what it tells us.

Do not confuse plot summary with interpretation. It may be necessary to summarize what happens in a story, but this is only preliminary to interpretation.

Assume that the human characters in a Bible story are our representatives. What happens to them also happens to us. What the disciples learn in the story we have been discussing is a lesson that we also need to learn.

Make sure that the main theme or meaning that you find in a story concerns the central aspect of the story. Many details in a story are "stage props"—details necessary to the action but not part of the main theme of the story.

Do not allegorize or spiritualize a story by translating the details into another set of meanings. This is not how stories work. In the story of the storm on the Sea of Galilee, the storm is a storm, not an allegory for Satan or Evil.

Avoiding Some Common Pitfalls

Along with all the things we should do with the stories of the Bible is an infamous list of things to avoid. Some teachers, for example, never enter the world of the biblical story. They try to move at once to the level of spiritual principles or application. Others try to deal with a story without talking about it as a story—in terms of setting, character, and action.

Faced with the need to fill the time, teachers who do not know how to enter the world of the story and talk about it in narrative terms have generated a list of fraudulent substitutes. One is to allegorize or spiritualize the story, turning details in the story into a corresponding meaning instead of allowing them to be literal phenomena. Mere plot summary is an old favorite, as is verse-by-verse moralizing. Yet another practice consists of taking students on a bicycle trip through parallel passages in the Bible.

If failure to enter the world of a biblical story is an abuse, the opposite is also possible. Some teachers assemble the details of the story with great flourish but do not move from the story to its meaning. They are interested in what happened to the disciples on the lake but not in how it applies to our own lives. Uninterpreted biblical narrative is a common failure.

The chief solution to these problems is the principle of bridging the gap between the ancient biblical world, with characters and customs remote from our own, and the modern world. On the one hand, we are almost always aware as we read the stories of the Bible of what a different world the biblical world is. We should begin by accepting the strangeness of that world. Abraham rode camels rather than airplanes, and we should not obscure this fact. But the events in the story of Abraham have correspondences to events in our own world.

The gap between the world of a biblical story and our own world can be bridged in the ways mentioned in an earlier chapter on the subject—by translating details from the story into their modern counterparts, by identifying the recognizable human experiences in the story, and by applying the principles of a biblical story to our own lives. The following excerpt successfully bridges the gap between the story of Abraham and Sarah in Genesis and our own world:

> They had gotten off to a good start in Mesopotamia. They had a nice house in the suburbs with a two-car garage and color TV and a barbecue pit. They had a room all fixed up for when the babies started coming.... Abraham was pulling down an excellent salary for a young man, plus generous fringe benefits.... And then they got religion, or religion got them, and Abraham was convinced that what God wanted them to do was pull up stakes and head out for Canaan.... They put the house on the market and gave the color TV to the hospital and got a good price for the crib and the bassinet because they had never been used and were good as new.... So off they went in their station wagon with a U-haul behind and a handful of friends and relations....[1]

This piece of commentary does not, of course, do all that we have recommended for biblical stories. But it illustrates the twin tendencies that are essential for good teaching of biblical narrative—the impulse to relive the experiences of the characters in a story and to feel what those experiences are like in our lives.

1. Frederick Buechner, *Telling the Truth: The Gospel as Tragedy, Comedy, and Fairy Tale* (San Francisco: Harper and Row, 1977), pp. 50–51.

13

Teaching the Poetry of the Bible

The Lord is my shepherd."
"You are the salt of the earth."
"Their tongue struts through the earth."
It is obvious that poets speak a language all their own. Because poetry is different from ordinary speech, it intimidates some people. Biblical poetry can become accessible if we simply learn a few rules that govern the writing and interpretation of poetry.

Mastering poetry is a requirement, not an option, for readers and teachers of the Bible. Poetry is simply too pervasive in the Bible to avoid. Some books of the Bible are wholly poetic: Psalms, the Song of Solomon, Proverbs, and Lamentations. Others are mainly poetic, such as Job, Ecclesiastes, Isaiah, and numerous other prophetic books.

But even parts of the Bible that are written in prose use the resources of poetic language, especially figures of speech. The most heavily theological parts of the Bible, such as the New Testament epistles, make continuous use of poetic language: "But God, who is rich in mercy . . . even when we were dead through our trespasses, made us alive together with Christ" (Eph. 2:4–5).

There is no need to be frightened by the prospect of teaching biblical poetry. Any effective teacher can learn to teach it with confidence. Doing so requires that we know what things make up poetry and the corresponding interpretive activities that these ask us to perform. This chapter will devote separate discussion to these poetic ingredients, with a concluding section on how poems are structured.

Thinking in Images

The most elementary thing to note about poetry is also the most important: poets think in images. No matter what the subject, the poetic imagination quickly turns it into a picture. Depression and loneliness, for example, become this in the hands of a poet:

> My heart is smitten like grass, and withered;
>   I forget to eat my bread.
> Because of my loud groaning
>   my bones cleave to my flesh.
> I am like a vulture of the wilderness,
>   like an owl of the waste places;
> I lie awake,
>   I am like a lonely bird on the housetop.
>   [Ps. 102:4–7]

For the poet, the experience of trusting God is a series of pictures:

> To thee I lift up my eyes,
>   O thou who are enthroned in the heavens!
> Behold, as the eyes of servants
>   look to the hand of their master,
> as the eyes of a maid
>   to the hand of her mistress,
> so our eyes look to the Lord our God,
>   till he have mercy upon us. [Ps. 123:1–2]

The poets are the photographers of the Bible. They appeal primarily to our imaginations—our image-making and image-perceiving capacity. In terms popularized by modern brain research, poetry is right-brain discourse.

When we ask classes to list the things that make up the content of the Psalms, the resulting list looks something like this: forgiveness, praise, depression, trust, providence, worship, godliness, and deliverance. This is a decidedly "left-brain" list—abstract, theological, and general. But an equally accurate list of what we encounter in the Psalms is this: thunder, honey, grass, frost, horse, dog, rock, and sword. In fact, the actual vocabulary of the Psalms is much closer to the second list.

[In poetry] the appeal is...to my senses....From Homer, who never omits to tell us that the ships were black and the sea salt, or even wet, down to Eliot with his "hollow valley" and "multi-foliate rose,"...poets are always telling us that grass is green, or thunder loud, or lips red. [Poetry] is not, except in bad poets, always telling us that things are shocking or delightful....To say that things were blue, or hard, or cool, or foul-smelling, or noisy, is to tell how they affected our senses.

C. S. Lewis, "The Language of Religion," in *Christian Reflections* (Grand Rapids: Eerdmans, 1967), pp. 131–32.

The images of biblical poetry require three main activities from us as readers and teachers. The images of poetry must first of all be *experienced* as images. We need to see and hear and touch what the poet names. The more concrete these images become in our imagination, the richer will be our encounter with poetic passages in the Bible.

In addition to simply experiencing poetic images, we need to interpret them. The simplest form of interpretation is to note the connotations of images. We must go beyond the denotative dictionary meaning of a word to the overtones and emotional associations that have grown around a word. The word *refuge* (Ps. 46:1) denotes a military stronghold such as a fort, but it connotes safety, protection, security, and deliverance. At the very least, we have to determine whether the connotations of an image in its context are positive or negative. Often there are additional connotations as well.

Thirdly, in additon to reliving an image and determining its connotations, we need to think about what a modern poet has called "the logic of images." That is, we can profitably meditate on why a poet has used a particular image where it appears. Why this image here? is a good question to ask regarding poetic images. Why do we find images of flooding and bird traps in a psalm about a nation that faced destruction? Because these are heightened images of terror and helplessness from the poet's experience. We need to look for the principle of suitability or fitness between a biblical poet's images and subject matter.

Practical Suggestions

> Because poetry consists of images, effective teaching of biblical poetry requires that we experience the images. Teachers should carry appropriate sensory objects to class, no matter how rudimentary or simple they might seem. If poets think in images, so must readers of poetry.

> Pictures and slides of images named in poetry are likewise invaluable tools in teaching poetry. Poetry is right-brain discourse. We therefore need to assimilate it with the right side of our brain, that is, as images.

> It is also important to operate on the premise that images are a very affective form of discourse. Images tend to awaken feelings within us. When teaching poetry, we should encourage rather than stifle affective responses.

> Try to counter the usual assumption that poetry is an unnatural, "difficult" form of discourse. In the history of civilizations, poetry precedes the development of prose. It is actually a simpler form of discourse than propositional prose. Once students realize this, they will begin to feel comfortable with poetry.

A Language of Comparison

The second most important principle of poetry is that it is based on a principle of comparison. The commonest form of figurative speech in poetry is to say that A is in some sense like B. The technical terms for the two figures of speech that compare things are *metaphor* and *simile*. A simile uses the formula *like* or *as* to express the comparison: He is like a tree planted by streams of water. A metaphor adopts a bolder strategy. It dispenses with the explicit "like" or "as" and asserts that one thing *is* another: The Lord is my shepherd.

Anger is expressed in Hebrew in a throng of ways, each picturesque, and each borrowed from physiological facts....*Discouragement* and *despair* are expressed by the melting of the heart, *fear* by the loosening of the reins. *Pride* is portrayed by the holding high of the head, with the figure straight and stiff....*Pardon* is expressed by a throng of metaphors borrowed from the idea of covering, of hiding, of coating over the fault. In *Job* God sews up sins in a sack, seals it, then throws it behind him: all to signify that he forgets them.

Ernest Renan, as quoted in J. H. Gardiner, *The Bible as English Literature* (New York: Scribner's, 1906), p. 114.

Both simile and metaphor assert a similarity between two things. They are split-level or bifocal statements. They ask us to bring two things into view. There is a picture side to these comparisons and a thinking side in which we have to analyze how the two phenomena are similar.

It is not hard to see what activities such comparisons require of us as readers and teachers. We must begin with the picture side. Before we determine how God's Word is like a lamp to our feet (Ps. 119:105), we need to picture a person walking in darkness with the aid of a lamp. A lot of commentary and Bible teaching leaps at once to interpreting the comparison. This common procedure is wrong. A simile or metaphor is an image before it is a comparison.

Having experienced one-half of the comparison—level A, let us call it—we have to transfer one or more meanings to the other half—level B—of the comparison. The very word *metaphor* suggests this. It is based on the Greek words *meta*, meaning "over," and *pherein*, meaning "to carry." In the metaphoric statement that "the Lord God is a sun and shield" (Ps. 84:11), we first have to let the literal picture of sun and shield sink into our consciousness. But we cannot stop there. We also have to interpret what qualities of sun and shield the poet intends us to carry over to our understanding of the nature of God. More often than not, the connections are multiple.

Metaphor and simile are forms of logic. The connection that a poet sets up between two things is subject to validation on the basis of observation and rational analysis. When a biblical poet claims that the godly person is like a tree planted by streams of water that produces fruit

---

The Hebrew language...expressed emotion always by naming the sensations of which the emotion consists....Often the emotion, instead of being set forth by the bodily sensation that constitutes it, is indirectly portrayed by naming the concrete objects which inevitably produce these sensations....The unsurpassed vividness of the Hebrew poetry and its unfailing hold on our imagination may be ascribed to this fact, that it always expressed emotions directly and concretely through sensations instead of describing them by words which are abstract and therefore pale.

We may go even further, and find in this special characteristic of the Hebrew language the cause for the permanent appeal of these ancient poems. The great body of our sensations and feelings does not change from generation to generation. The horror of despair at sinking into deep mire, the dread at the creeping mysteries of the night, of the delight in uttering forth our joy in song, all are the same thing for us to-day that they were for these ancient Hebrews two thousand years ago....Thus a literature which is able to express itself through these inalterable sensations has a permanence of power impossible to any literature which is phrased largely in abstractions.

J. H. Gardiner, *The Bible as English Literature* (New York: Scribner's, 1906), pp. 116–21.

---

in its season (Ps. 1:3), we can validate the statement by examining the logic of the connection. Despite what might appear to be the far-flung fantasy of the imagination, poets use a form of logic when they speak in metaphor and simile.

The comparisons of metaphor and simile are more than poetic embellishment. They are ways of understanding reality and expressing truth. They are based on the premise that we can use one area of experience to cast light on another area. There really is something about human fathers that expresses a truth about God that cannot be expressed in the same way by prose abstraction. If we understand that this language of comparison is a way of understanding, we will not be surprised that similes and metaphors occur throughout the Bible, not simply in the poetic books.

Practical Suggestions

Metaphors and similes place immense demands on readers and teachers. The fact that they require us to carry over the meaning from one thing to another means that they are an *invitation to discover* the writer's or speaker's meaning. The poet's meaning is not complete until the interpreter performs the transfer of meaning from one level to another. Knowing this, and despite the fact that we can of course make mistakes in the process of interpretation, we should be bold in interpreting metaphors and similes. In giving us the Bible, God thought the risk worth taking.

Do not be misled by commentaries that neglect the descriptive task of constructing the literal picture and that want to get at once to the meaning of a simile or metaphor. The methodology of these commentaries is simply wrong. You can use them in the transfer phase of interpretation, but you will need to follow your own intuitions in painting the literal picture. Commentaries should contain far more photographic commentary than they do. As teacher, you can often supply such commentary from sources other than commentaries, especially Bible dictionaries.

Metaphor and simile are meditative forms. They force us to ponder a statement and analyze the connections that the poet intends us to draw between two phenomena. Far from being a liability, this is actually an asset to Bible teaching. In an inductive study, the whole group can contribute to the interpretive process of discovering the meaning of a metaphor or simile. By forcing us to pause on a statement, moreover, metaphor and simile encourage us to read the Bible in keeping with its meditative purpose, for surely we would agree that the point in reading or studying a Bible passage is not to get finished as quickly as possible so we can move on to something else.

Several curbs can be applied to the interpretation of similes and metaphors. They include common sense, logical validation of the connections between the two phenomena that are joined in the poet's statement, and a consensus among reliable commentators.

Poetry as a Form of Fiction

Our discussion of the images and comparisons that make up biblical poetry has anticipated this section on poetry as a form of fiction. A metaphor, for example, is always a literal lie in the sense that it asserts something that is not literally true. Christians are not literally salt and light. God is not literally a shepherd, nor are people sheep. Poetry is inherently fictional.

Even the images and similes of poetry illustrate this, though not so directly as metaphors do. Biblical poems are filled with images, but the poems are not really *about* these images. Psalm 1, for example, gives us the images of pathway, streams, trees, chaff, and courtroom. But the poem is not about any of these things. It is about the lives of godly and wicked people. Biblical poets operate on the premise of "it is as if"—it is as if the godly person is like a tree, eventual judgment is like receiving a sentence in a courtroom, and life itself is like walking down a path.

Some additional figures of speech that we encounter in biblical poetry reinforce the principle that poetry is a form of fiction rather than literal statement. One of these figures is *hyperbole*. Hyperbole is conscious exaggeration for the sake of effect. The Bible is filled with such statements: "my tears have been my food / day and night" (Ps. 42:3); "my enemies trample upon me all day long" (Ps. 56:2); "when you give to the needy, do not let your left hand know what your right hand is doing" (Matt. 6:3 NIV).

What is the point of such exaggerations? Often they are a way of expressing strong feeling. In such cases, they express emotional truth rather than literal truth. They communicate how the speaker feels about a matter. In other instances, such as Jesus' statement about not letting our right hand know what our left hand is doing, hyperbole highlights a truth in such a striking way that we will take note of it. Hyperbole is heightened speech. The main interpretive principle that emerges from this is that we should never try to take a hyperbolic statement literally.

Personification is another fictional device that poets love to use. It consists of treating something nonhuman (and perhaps even inanimate) as though it were a person: "righteousness and peace will kiss each other" (Ps. 85:10); "Oh send out thy light and thy truth; / let them lead me" (Ps. 43:3); "after desire has conceived, it gives birth to sin; and sin, when it is full-grown, gives birth to death" (James 1:15 NIV).

Personification is chiefly a way of making an abstraction concrete and vivid. As interpreters, we mainly have to recognize that personification is a form of poetic license—something that is not literally true but that expresses truth vividly in a fictional way. The spiritual qualities of righteousness and peace are not literally persons who can kiss each other; this is simply a piece of make-believe by which the poet expresses the truth that these qualities will exist together in God's coming kingdom. Sin does not literally give birth to death; this is a bit of poetic license by which the writer communicates how sin, if left unchecked, naturally and inevitably produces spiritual death. Such poetic license overcomes the clichéd effect of familiar ideas and is much more memorable than ordinary ways of speaking.

Apostrophe is yet another figure of speech that uses fiction. It consists of a direct address to someone or something absent as though it were present. Impassioned language regularly employs such addresses. We find it, for example, in poetry: "Depart from me, all you workers of evil" (Ps. 6:8); "Lift up your heads, O you gates" (Ps. 24:7 NIV). Such fictional addresses are equally characteristic of impassioned prose: "O death, where is thy victory?"

(1 Cor. 15:55); "O Jerusalem, Jerusalem, you who kill the prophets and stone those sent to you" (Matt. 23:37 NIV).

In real life people do not address objects and absent people in this way. Unless we recognize the inherently fictional nature of such utterances, we will think them rather silly. They are one of the fictional conventions of poetic speech. Beyond this, apostrophes are a sure sign that the speaker or writer is expressing strong feeling about a subject.

To sum up, the Bible contains an abundance of figurative speech. It clusters in poetic parts of the Bible, but it is not limited to them. To respond to poetry, we need the right antennae by which to assimilate its messages. Figurative speech is inherently fictional. If you or your students do not recognize this, you will not feel comfortable with poetry. As long as we have antennae only for literal statements, we will be continuously frustrated with the figurative language of the Bible, which is much more than a literal book.

Practical Suggestions

Evangelical Christians have done a great disservice by popularizing the motto that they "interpret the Bible literally." *No one* interprets the whole Bible literally. The Bible is filled with figurative statements that are not literally true. Jesus is not literally bread, light, or a door. In fact, it is so misleading to speak of interpreting the Bible literally that we should call a moratorium on this statement and find a more accurate substitute by which to denote believing that the historical and supernatural statements of the Bible are factually true (except when they are phrased in obviously figurative terms).

The standard word by which literary people refer to the unrealistic element of figurative language is "poetic license." It is not an inaccurate term, but is by itself incomplete. It is important to establish that figurative language is essentially *fictional* rather than factual or literal. Some people will find it liberating to know that poetic language is fictional, since it will confirm what they always suspected but perhaps did not know how to phrase. Other people will find it threatening to be told that there is a fictional element in the Bible. Do not back down on the issue in the face of such people. To make sense of the Bible we need to know that it often uses fiction—things not literally or factually true—to express the truth.

In addition to identifying a figurative statement as fictional rather than literal, it is always legitimate to ask what the specific function of a given figure of speech is in its context. The first two sections of this chapter suggested how images, similes, and metaphors are used to communicate reality and express truth. The three figures of speech on which we have focused in this section—hyperbole, personification, and apostrophe—usually serve two main functions. One is to express emotional intensity (or emotional truth). They can also be used to highlight a subject so we see the issues more clearly. In either case, we must always remember that poetry is heightened speech. It is an other-than-ordinary way of speaking and as such has an ability both to capture our attention and express aspects of experience.

How Poems Are Organized

As we have suggested, understanding biblical poetry first of all requires that we know how to interact with figurative language. But we also need to understand how poems are organized. An expository passage is structured as a flow of ideas. A story is organized as a succession of related episodes or events.

Poems are a more mixed form. They need to be divided into units on the basis of as many as three ingredients—ideas, feelings, or images. Regardless of which of these are important in a given poem, the best framework to have in mind when dividing a poem into an outline is the framework of theme and variation. The theme is the main idea that governs the poem. The variations on that theme—the specific ways in which the poet develops the theme—are the subordinate sections into which we can divide the poem. Dividing a poem into its parts is an essential step in showing the unity of the poem.

To illustrate how a poem is structured, we have selected Psalm 1. We should note in advance that the degree of specificity with which we divide a poem depends on how much time we plan to spend on the poem in a given teaching session and the tolerance for detail that our audience possesses. The following analysis strikes a balance between being general and very specific.

Psalm 1 begins by announcing the theme of the poem: *"Blessed is the man...."* We now know that the poem will be a meditation on the blessedness of the godly person. Having introduced the big idea around which he will build the poem, the poet's first variation is a series of three parallel statements that list the activities that the godly person avoids:

> who walks not in the counsel of the wicked,
>   nor stands in the way of sinners,
>   nor sits in the seat of scoffers.

We know that these lines belong together because they are similar in topic (what the godly person does not do) and are further joined by the parallelism of Hebrew poetry (in which the poet says the same thing more than once in similar grammatical form).

The poet's second variation on his theme of the blessedness of the godly person is a contrasting picture of what the godly person does positively:

> but his delight is in the law of the Lord,
>   and on his law he meditates day and night.

To complete his portrait of the godly person, the poet presents a third variation on the theme, consisting of an extended simile in which the godly person is compared to a fruitful tree:

> He is like a tree
>   planted by streams of water,
> that yields its fruit in its season,
>   and its leaf does not wither.
> In all that he does, he prospers.

We might note that the principle by which we isolate these lines into a unit is not so much idea as image. This reminds us that poems are a language of images as well as ideas.

The next variation on the main theme of Psalm 1 is a variation-by-contrast in which the blessedness of the godly person is opposed to the worthlessness of the wicked:

> the wicked are not so,
>   but are like chaff which the wind drives away.

On the basis of imagery, we can separate this comparison of the wicked to chaff from the next two lines, which take us to the world of the courtroom or assembly:

> Therefore the wicked will not stand in the judgment,
>   nor sinners in the congregation of the righteous.

The final variation is a summing up of the double message of the whole poem—the blessedness of the godly person as contrasted to the judgment of the wicked:

> for the LORD knows the way of the righteous,
>   but the way of the wicked will perish.

When we come to divide a poetic passage into its structural units, our best ally is the framework of theme and variation. It is an analytic framework that we can always impose on a poetic passage. We are never in the position of being able to do no more than paraphrase a poem (restate the poem in our own words).

Psalm 1 illustrates other key principles by which poetic passages are organized. One is the principle of contrast. It is always wise to ask whether a given poem is organized around one or more contrasts, such as that between the blessedness of the godly and the judgment of the wicked in Psalm 1.

Most poems also follow the principle of three-part construction. They begin with an indication of the controlling theme. They then develop that theme by means of specific variations. At the end, poets round off their composition with a note of resolution or finality. It is also useful to know that many psalms, including all of the psalms of praise, use the list or catalogue as an organizing principle.

Practical Suggestions

The principle by which we divide a poem into its units is to put "like with like." Lines that deal with the same topic or employ the same imagery should be put together and separated from lines that deal with other subject matter or imagery. Because Psalm 1 is a meditative poem, we divided it into units on the basis of either idea or image. In more emotional poems, a third element often becomes the basis for identifying a unit, namely, the feeling that is expressed.

Dividing a poem into its structural units serves several essential functions. It shows the unity of the poem and as such allows us to see the poem as a whole. By organizing the poem into its sequential units, moreover, we have the right organizing framework by which to progress through the poem as we discuss it. Dividing the poem into its parts is also a helpful analytic process while coming to understand the poem. Because it serves necessary functions, laying out a poetic passage into its constituent parts is a requirement, not an option, when teaching poetic parts of the Bible.

As you determine to your satisfaction where the divisions of a poem fall, you should draw horizontal lines in the text with a pencil. This allows you to visualize the movement of the poem and saves you the work of having to do this analytic process again. If you use a pencil, you can always change your mind if your understanding of the poem changes.

When we see a good outline of a poem, the process of laying out the units of a poem seems simple and easy. Our experience is that the ability to outline a biblical poem is an acquired skill. People who do it for the first time mystify us with some of their divisions. The best rule to follow is to stare at a poem carefully and make sure that divisions are based on the logic of putting "like with like" in the areas of topic, emotion, or image.

14

Teaching Other Genres of the Bible

Story and poetry are the two dominant forms in the Bible. Knowing how to interact with stories and poems is the initial requirement for teaching the Bible well. But this knowledge is insufficient by itself. At least five additional types of writing in the Bible are sufficiently different from story and poetry that we need to know something about them.

The Proverb

A proverb is a concise, memorable statement of truth. The writers of the Bible used the word *saying* to name this form. It is a major form in the Bible. Wisdom literature such as the Book of Proverbs consists wholly of proverbs. Much of the teaching of Jesus is likewise in the form of sayings. But the Bible as a whole is the most proverbial book in the Western world. We continuously need to know how to interpret proverbs in order to understand its message.

The Proverb as a Literary Form

Proverbs have several distinguishing characteristics. We can begin by noting the purpose of a proverb. A

proverb is part of the human *urge for order*. The author of
a proverb wants to make a vast area of life understandable
by bringing it under the control of a universal principle
that explains it. Proverbs organize our understanding
about life by bringing a given area of experience into
focus. A proverb is an insight into the repeatable situations of life, an observation about how things are in the
world.

Proverbs are also *striking and memorable*. They not
only express insight into life—they are often so striking
that they actually compel such insight, as in the statement, "He who loves money will not be satisfied with
money" (Eccles. 5:10). A proverb attempts to overcome
the clichéd effect of statements or ideas. By stating the
truth in such striking and memorable form, a proverb
forces us to take notice. Having heard a proverb, we are
inclined to carry it with us into life, to examine its meaning, and to apply it. It is important to note in this regard
that a good proverb does not put an end to thought and
application but actually encourages them.

The essence of a proverbial saying is that it is based on observation of
how things are in the world. It is a flash of insight into the repeatable
situations of life in the world, and its aphoristic form not only represents
insight but also compels it. . . . In the context of a firm belief in God, the
proverb comes to express insight into the way things are, or should be, in
the world ordered by God and a challenge to behavior that God will reward.

Norman Perrin, *The New Testament: An Introduction* (New York: Harcourt Brace
Jovanovich, 1974), p. 296.

Proverbs are simultaneously *simple and profound*.
They are short and easily grasped on the surface. To be
told that "a man reaps what he sows" (Gal. 6:7 NIV) should
baffle no one. But proverbs are also profound. They usually touch upon the basic issues of life, so that their very
seriousness and universality make them profound. Furthermore, proverbs are open-ended in their application, so

that the significance of what looks like a simple idea is never exhausted.

Something else to notice about proverbs is that they are often *poetic in form*. They often use concrete images, for example: "Through sloth the roof sinks in" (Eccles. 10:18). Metaphor and simile appear frequently: "The path of the righteous is like the light of dawn" (Prov. 4:18). Paradox is frequent in Jesus' sayings: "My yoke is easy and my burden is light" (Matt. 11:30 NIV). Whenever a proverb uses figurative language, we must apply all that was said about poetic language in the previous chapter.

Finally, proverbs are often *specific and universal at the same time*. They give us specific pictures of universal principles. The proverb "through sloth the roof sinks in" is talking about more than houses; it is a comment about sloth in any area of life. Similarly, the statement that "in the place where the tree falls, there it will lie" (Eccles. 11:3) is more than a simple-minded observation about felling trees. It uses a concrete picture to express an insight into the element of finality that characterizes many of our experiences in life.

Teaching the Proverbs of the Bible

The chief difficulty to overcome when teaching the proverbs of the Bible stems from their brevity and self-contained nature. A proverb is complete in itself. It is an insight into life, separated, however, from its life context. A proverb organizes reality, but *we* have to provide the data from life that it organizes. In fact, the place where a proverb comes to life is the everyday situation where it applies.

A primary task when we teach the proverbs of the Bible is thus to supply a context from life that illustrates a given proverb. Teachers do not have the wealth of experience to provide that context by themselves, though their own experiences and observations are of course the starting place. Teachers need to draw upon the combined experiences of a class to construct a context from real life or the daily news.

It is important to note that the proverb is a meditative form. It invites us to pause and consider it carefully. It is entirely appropriate to proceed slowly when teaching proverbs, taking the time to think about how they apply to life.

Another part of the interpretive task is to determine whether a proverb is descriptive or prescriptive—whether it merely describes how things are or expresses something that we are expected to follow in our lives. Sometimes a proverb is an observation about what happens in the world: "Because sentence against an evil deed is not executed speedily, the heart of the sons of men is fully set to do evil" (Eccles. 8:11). This is not an invitation to license. It is simply an observation about what goes wrong in our world when justice is administered slowly. Similarly, to say that "one sinner destroys much good" (Eccles. 9:18) is to make an observation, not to prescribe something.

Sometimes the proverbs of the Bible actually express an immoral viewpoint—not with approval, but simply as an acknowledgment of what prevails in the world. For example, the comment that "money is the answer for everything" (Eccles. 10:19 NIV), equivalent to our saying that "money talks," states what happens—but should not happen—in our world.

Other proverbs are obviously prescriptions for how we are expected to live as moral and godly people. In fact, many proverbs are stated in the form of commands: "Do not wear yourself out to get rich" (Prov. 23:4 NIV).

The process of distinguishing between descriptive and prescriptive proverbs is more complex than it may seem, for the following reason: *many proverbs that express observations actually prescribe a mode of behavior.* Observational proverbs tend to be implied comments about good and bad behavior—about virtues and vices. For every proverb, therefore, we should ask, What type of behavior does this proverb encourage or prohibit?

Consider the following verses from Proverbs 27:

> [6]Faithful are the wounds of a friend;
> profuse are the kisses of an enemy.

> [14]He who blesses his neighbor with a loud voice,
> rising early in the morning,
> will be counted as cursing.

> [15]A continual dripping on a rainy day
> and a contentious woman are alike.

These are stated as observations, but they actually push us in the direction of certain types of behavior. Verse 6 encourages honesty and discourages flattery or hypocrisy. Verse 14 implies that being considerate of other people is a virtue. Verse 15 is a warning against nagging.

Practical Suggestions

Successful teaching of proverbs requires that students live with the proverbs before coming to class. The best strategy is to parcel out specific proverbs to individual class members the week before the lesson. Alternately, the whole passage can be assigned to the entire class. In any event, people have to devote some time to collecting their real-life illustrations or applications for proverbs.

Newspapers and news magazines are also sources of data to illustrate proverbs. The basic principle to remember is that proverbs are observations about life.

Proverbs lend themselves to photographic illustration, in the form of either slides or collages. Robert Short's book *A Time to Be Born—A Time to Die* (New York: Harper and Row, 1973), which provides photographic commentary on the Book of Ecclesiastes, shows what can be done along these lines.

Be sure to explore whether proverbs that are stated as observations are actually prescriptive in their tendency to encourage certain types of behavior and discourage other types.

Satire

Satire is the exposure of human vice or folly through ridicule or rebuke. It has four ingredients, and these are the framework of considerations that a teacher should bring to bear on any satiric passage.

The Ingredients of Satire

The thing that identifies a passage as a satire is *an object of attack*. This object of attack is usually a recognizable historical particular—particular people or groups (such as the Pharisees), institutions (religious or governmental), or practices (such as the luxurious living financed by exploitation of the poor [Amos 4:1; 5:11]). Occasionally the object of satiric attack is not a historical particular but something universal, such as greed or pride.

The satiric attack is always embodied in a *satiric vehicle*. This might be something as simple as a single metaphor or simile, as when Jesus attacks the Pharisees with the statement, "You are like whitewashed tombs, which outwardly appear beautiful, but within...are full of dead men's bones and all uncleanness" (Matt. 23:27). Another common satiric vehicle in the Bible is the oracle of judgment—a denunciation of evil and prediction of calamity spoken by God's prophets. Here is a typical oracle of judgment from an Old Testament prophetic book:

> Woe to those who are heroes at drinking wine,
>   and valiant men in mixing strong drink,
> who acquit the guilty for a bribe,
>   and deprive the innocent of his right!
> Therefore, as the tongue of fire devours the stubble,
>   and as dry grass sinks down in the flame,
> so their root will be as rottenness,
>   and their blossom go up like dust. [Isa. 5:22–24]

Narrative or story is also prominent as a satiric vehicle in the Bible. Many of Jesus' parables, such as those of the rich man and Lazarus and the Pharisee and tax collector, are satiric. The Old Testament Book of Jonah is an example of an extended satiric story. Many of the Old Testament histories of individuals are satiric exposures of the protagonist's failings.

Every satire also has a stated or implied *satiric norm*. This is the standard of goodness against which the object of attack is measured. Usually a satiric passage contains some hint of the ideal within its picture of what is wrong. In the parable of the Pharisee and tax collector, for example, the humility of the repentant tax collector is the standard by which we judge the self-righteous pride of the Pharisee. Sometimes the satiric norm is something we have to infer. In the passage from Isaiah, for example, we infer that the justice of God is the standard by which the drunkard and dishonest judge will be condemned.

Finally, pieces of satire have a discernible *tone*. Satire is either biting or light. It either lashes out at vice or folly, or it laughs at them.

Overall, we can say that satire is a subversive genre. It aims to assault our complacency. The satirist is a bearer of bad tidings.

The Scope of Satire in the Bible

Satire is a major biblical form, even though there are few books that are wholly satiric. Satire is a common element in the stories of the Bible, for example. In the stories of Genesis, the character flaws of Abraham and Jacob are held up to satiric exposure. In the story of Esther, Haman's pride is satirized. In the Gospels, the religious establishment is a nearly constant object of satiric rebuke.

Satire is one of the most helpful frameworks for dealing with the frequently unwieldy Old Testament prophetic books. These kaleidoscopic books keep shifting from one subject to another. The two commonest types of material are the oracle of judgment that predicts woe and the oracle of redemption that forecasts God's mercy. The best framework for interacting with the oracles of judgment is satire. We can identify an object of attack and a satiric vehicle, norm, and tone.

Satire also appears in the poetry and proverbs of the Bible. In the Psalms, for example, we find satiric portraits of the speaker's enemies in the lament psalms, as well as taunt songs that mock the worshipers of idols. As for satiric proverbs, consider these specimens: "He who meddles in a quarrel not his own is like one who takes a passing dog by the ears" (Prov. 26:17); "A continual dripping on a rainy day and a contentious woman are alike" (Prov. 27:15).

Practical Suggestions

Because satire is usually an attack on historical particulars, one has to recover the historical context that will explain what the writer is attacking. A certain amount of research thus becomes a requirement for teaching much of the satire of the Bible.

Having established the original context of a satiric passage, you must bridge the gap by determining what aspects of your own society are represented by the persons or practices attacked in a satiric passage. For example, Who are the Pharisees of our day? Who are the Jonahs of today?

One of the best ways to show the contemporaneity of Old Testament prophetic satire is to collect visual pictures or news items that "update" the details in the text. The Book of Amos, for example, lends itself to slides that picture modern counterparts to the things that the prophet attacks.

Visionary Writing

The complexity of visionary writing in the Bible is such that the temptation is great to omit it from discussions like this. Yet so much of the Bible falls into this genre that any Bible teacher needs to confront it.

Visionary writing transports us to a strange world where the ordinary laws of earthly existence are suspended. It presents us with a vision of something other than current reality. The opening verses of Zechariah 5, for example, describe a flying scroll that destroys the houses of thieves and people who swear falsely. Revelation 13 describes a beast that arises out of the sea, speaks like a dragon, and performs great signs that deceive people on earth.

What are we supposed to do with passages like these? The first requirement is to allow ourselves to be transported into the strange world that is presented to us. Visionary writing is a form of fantasy. It demands first to be taken on its own terms, which of course have an element of strangeness. Most visionary writing in the Bible puts something before us that is not factually true, whether at the time the writer spoke or in our world at any point in time.

Visionary literature is also right-brain discourse. It is filled with images. These images appeal to our sense of mystery rather than our sense of literal fact. Such writing is intuitive and affective, not primarily rational.

Not everyone likes this kind of writing, but this is no reason to avoid teaching it. For one thing, some people *do* resonate with visionary writing. We need to realize that many people find the heavy theology of Romans or Galatians difficult and inaccessible, too. Secondly, once people see how to interpret visionary writing they will find it less intimidating. The fear of visionary passages in the Bible is largely a fear of the unknown. Finally, the high incidence of such writing in the prophetic and apocalyptic parts of the Bible shows that God wants us to understand it.

How, then, should we interpret the strange details of visionary writing once we have experienced them? The rule of interpretation is really quite simple. We need to ask, Of what familiar theological fact or event in salvation history is this a picture? The strange images of visionary literature bring familiar realities to mind. The important principle to practice is relating the visionary details to familiar biblical teaching.

Visionary writing is folk literature. We need to go for the simple, obvious meaning. A flying scroll that devours evil people's houses is a picture of God's judgment against evil. The beast of Revelation 13 that works great signs and deceives people is a picture of the power of evil in the world. The familiar reality that it calls to mind is what Jesus described in the Olivet Discourse: "False Christs and false prophets will arise and show great signs and wonders, so as to lead astray, if possible, even the elect" (Matt. 24:24). Interpreting visionary literature is often as simple as this.

Much visionary writing is governed by the principle of symbolism. In such instances, things stand for something else. The picture of an angel tossing grapes into a wine-press, for example, symbolizes God's judgment against evil (Rev. 14:19). Garments of white linen symbolize the spiritual purity of the saints in heaven (Rev. 19:14). In all such instances, we realize that the images are not literally true, but they bring realities to mind.

Practical Suggestions

A teacher's attitude toward visionary literature influences how students view it. Do not make dire statements about how weird such writing is. Instead speak of it as folk literature that appeals to what is childlike in us. If you handle such passages with zest and confidence, you will convince most students that they, too, can interpret such writing.

Visionary literature has something of the riddle about it. Faced with the puzzle, people have a natural curiosity to discover what the details mean. This is an asset in Bible studies.

The chief difficulty with visionary writing in inductive Bible studies is finding adequate controls on the interpretations that students produce. The solution to the problem is for a leader to be well-prepared (which requires consulting several reputable commentaries) and willing to exercise firm leadership of the discussion.

The Epistles

Many Bible teachers gravitate naturally to the Epistles when they choose passages for study. After all, these are the most theological parts of the Bible. Because the Epistles are largely expository (explanatory) writing, they seem manageable.

It is necessary, however, to sound a cautionary note. Theological passages can become an occasion for controversy and unanswered questions. It is hard to stay within a given passage when dealing with a theological issue, and once a group starts tracking a theological idea through the Bible, things can really be up for grabs. Then, too, theological passages, being idea-oriented, can be very abstract. Once one has mastered the ideas in a theological passage, the only thing that remains to do is to believe and apply it. Bible studies dealing with passages from the Epistles are often quickly finished.

Our practical advice regarding the Epistles is threefold. First, since the Epistles are largely expository in form, we should look primarily for a structure of ideas. Most emphatically, we must "think paragraphs" when reading the Epistles. It is not so much the individual verse or sentence that conveys the meaning as the individual paragraph.

Secondly, although the Epistles consist of expository prose, they contain an abundance of figurative language scattered throughout the prose. The Holy Spirit, writes Paul, "is the guarantee of our inheritance until we acquire possession of it" (Eph. 1:14). We must interpret such figurative language in keeping with all that we know about poetic language (as discussed in the previous chapter).

Finally, the Epistles are "occasional" letters—letters that were prompted by specific occasions. They were addressed to specific people or congregations. They are not essays in systematic theology. Instead, the authors take up the questions or problems that have arisen in the lives of specific people or churches. The accompanying rule of interpretation is that we must avoid pressing the Epistles into more systematic form than was intended by the authors.

> Since these are letters, the points argued and stressed are often not those of the greatest importance. They are usually points about which differences of opinion existed....The churches addressed...knew [the author's] views on the great central facts; these he can take for granted. It is to show them their mistakes in the application of these central facts to their daily life, to help their doubts, that he writes....Many of the questions he discusses are those propounded by the perplexed church. He answers the question because it has been raised.
>
> Morton Scott Enslin, *The Literature of the Christian Movement* (New York: Harper and Row, 1938, 1956), p. 214.

Practical Suggestions

Because the Epistles frequently speak to specific situations in the author's life and time, it may be necessary to reconstruct the historical context. Sometimes an epistle will itself suggest this context, but consulting commentaries is essential for a teacher of the Epistles.

Once we have uncovered the original circumstances, we then face the interpretive problems of whether the author's statements still apply today. They usually do, but not always. As examples of the latter, we might note the rules for women being veiled in church (1 Cor. 11:2–6) or for slaves obeying their masters.

In other instances we must determine exactly how a given statement applies today. What, for example, is the modern counterpart of food offered to idols? Often we need to look for underlying principles in answering these questions.

The Parables

The parables of Jesus are stories, but they require specific interpretive activities beyond ordinary narrative considerations. A complete analysis of parables falls naturally into four phases, and these are also the best way to teach the parables.

We must begin with the parables as stories. This involves identifying and reliving the literal details—the images, settings, characters, and events. The parables are striking in their realism. They obey the rules of folk stories, such as conflict or contrast, repetition (often threefold repetition), end stress, universal character types, and the presence of archetypes (familiar images). The parables are too simple to interest us fully only at this level, but it is the necessary starting point.

> Now, of course, Jesus' thought moves on beyond the actual stories. They are only spring-boards or doors to something more important. There is the picture-side of the parable and there is the meaning or application. . . . Jesus is not merely clarifying difficult ideas. He is leading men to make a judgment and to come to a decision. The stories are so told as to compel men to see things as they are, by analogy. . . . And they do this by evoking men's everyday experience. It is implicit that a man can be saved where he is. And, indeed, the Gospel proposes not to substitute another world for this one, but to redeem and to transfigure the present world.
>
> Amos N. Wilder, *Early Christian Rhetoric* (Cambridge: Harvard University Press, 1971), pp. 74–75.

Secondly, we need to identify the details in the parables that are intended to be interpreted allegorically or symbolically. The essential technique in the parables is that of double meaning, as even the word *parable*—"to throw alongside"—suggests. In the parable of the sower, for example, the sowing of the seed is the preaching of the gospel, the various types of soil represent people who hear the gospel, and the types of harvest or nonharvest symbolize the range of responses by people who hear the gospel. Not all of the details in a parable are necessarily intended to be thus translated into another meaning, but some details in virtually all of the parables are intended to be interpreted symbolically.

Having identified the symbolic meanings, we need to identify the themes or ideas that a parable embodies. This is different from interpreting the symbolism. Having identified what the details in the parable of the sower mean, we must proceed to interpret the meaning of the parable as a whole. It embodies such ideas as these: the preaching of the gospel occurs in a context of spiritual warfare; the gospel will meet with resistance when it is preached; it will also produce fruit in the lives of some who hear; salvation depends on the responses of the people who hear the gospel.

Finally, we need to determine how the themes in a parable apply to people. We must begin with how the parable applied to the original audience. Then we can analyze how it applies today. Often the themes of a parable are sufficiently universal that the two applications are virtually the same. The parable of the sower falls into this category. One application is that we must have realistic expectations about the preaching of God's Word. Not everyone will respond positively to the gospel. On the other hand, we can be encouraged by the knowledge that some people will respond positively. The main application, though, is a challenge to obey the gospel. The main point of this parable is, Take care how you respond to God's Word.

Practical Suggestions

Several things make the parables a good choice for Bible studies. Their surface simplicity makes them accessible to people. Although they teach basic Christian theology, they do not possess the intimidating theological language or complexity of the Epistles.

The parables are the very epitome of the folk imagination as it has existed through the centuries. At the story level, they have many of the features of folk stories and fairy stories. These universal qualities should be pointed out to students.

Because many of the details in the parables also stand for something else, they are an invitation to discovery. As such, they are good at activating a class.

Index of Subjects

Index of Authors

255